IMAGE **ANISA MAKHOUL** ILLUSTRATION **SHUTTERSTOCK**

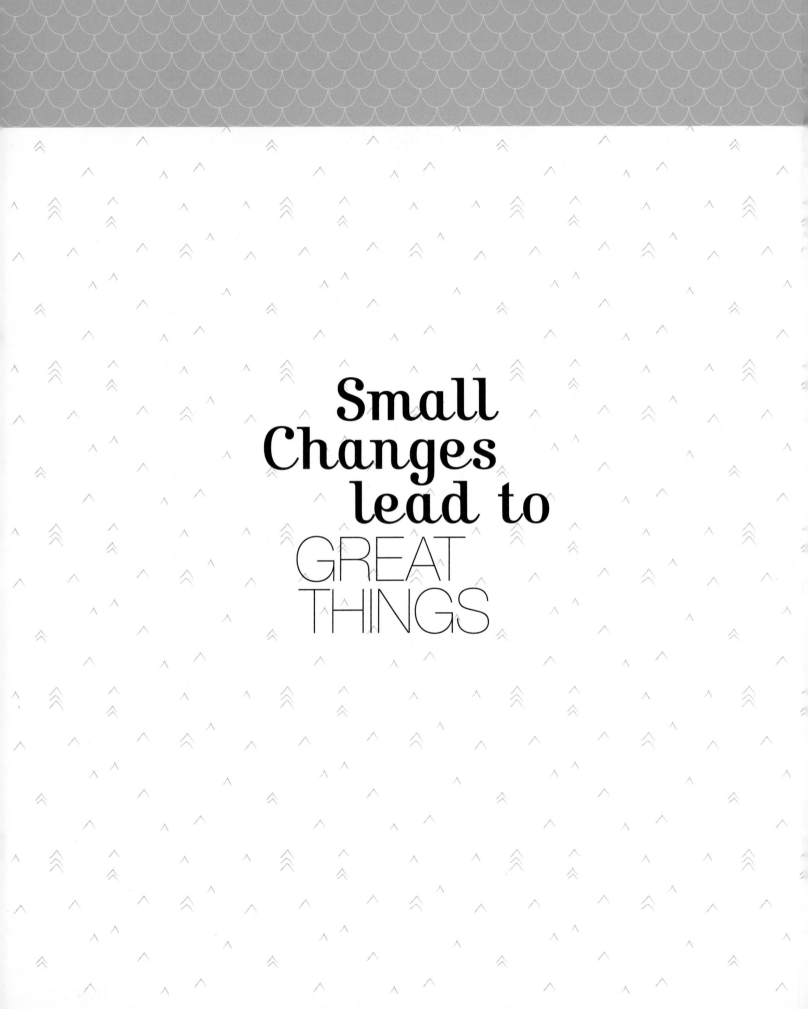

Editorial

If you've been paying any attention to us in recent years, you will know we don't exactly lead glitzy, glamorous lives. That doesn't mean we don't feel a little pang of jealousy now and then at those who do, though. We're sometimes envious of the kind of people who can say, 'Let's get in the car *right now* and drive to Paris'. Or those who casually throw a party for 300 friends. Or people who never say, 'I have to get up early tomorrow', but just go out all night without worrying about how they'll manage the next day.

We'd kind of like to emulate the way they live their lives, but you know what? Things are what they are, and we're just not like that.

And somehow, in a way, we find beauty in the way we are. Because enjoying what you have, being happy and able to appreciate an ordinary kind of week or an average Sunday can give a person a deep sense of satisfaction.

In short, we're more about small gestures and tiny tweaks than rigorous makeovers and extreme change. This edition of Flow acknowledges some of these small changes. Because we were in the mood for a little remodeling, and because we're celebrating the magazine's tenth anniversary this year. We want Flow to express even more vividly what it is: A magazine that celebrates slowing down, life's little pleasures and making choices. And making small changes can often lead to great things. We're delighted with our beautiful new cover and the new fonts inside. We've also shaken up the sections a little, and given them new names: 'Time', 'People' and 'Mind'. And we've added a new one—'Pictures'—which we're really happy with. This section doesn't rely on words, but on beautiful images, photography and illustrations instead. Because we believe that pictures do something to you. In our new series 'The Correspondent', Dutch foreign correspondents reveal something about the country they live in by telling us the stories they haven't shared before. And these are just a few of the new things you'll find inside this issue.

We are also very proud of our Flow Mini Course that will come in the form of a large workbook accompanying several issues of Flow in the coming year. Each workbook has a theme of its own, so when you have them all, you'll have a nice collection of life lessons to hand.

It's been a beautiful and exhilarating decade and we're delighted you've joined us on this amazing journey. Thank you.

Astrid & Irene

astrid@flowmagazine.com   irene@flowmagazine.com

You can follow us on flowmagazine.com, (flow_magazine), (Flow Magazine INT) and (Flow Magazine).

PHOTOGRAPHY DANIQUE VAN KESTEREN ILLUSTRATION SUZANNE NUIS

68

84

40

52

13

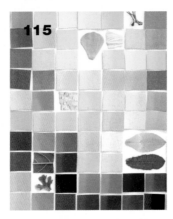
115

90

21

62

76

48

flow
contents

>> **HOW TO GET YOUR HANDS ON A COPY OF FLOW:**

Subscribe and get Flow delivered to you anywhere in the world. See page 28.

Order a copy online from our web shop: flowmagazine.com/shop.

Find a copy in your local store. Check flowmagazine.com/store-locator for stockists in the UK, US and Canada.

Missed an issue? You can also buy back issues of Flow from our web shop: flowmagazine.com/shop.

contents

PICTURES

LIFE

Four illustrated mini posters

FLOW EXTRAS

* **NEW FLOW MINI COURSE WORKBOOK**

* **MINI POSTERS** (Page 88)

Small Changes. Big Results

Behind the Scenes

See feature on page 110

MAKING MEMORIES

Journalist Hedwig Wiebes wrote the feature about anticipatory nostalgia for this issue: "Traveling full-time in a camper van, I come across lots of places that I am sad to leave, and perhaps will never return to. The strange thing is that I always feel this while I am still there, fully enjoying it. I've discovered that this bittersweet feeling actually has a purpose: It enables us to remember those nice moments extra well, so that they serve as a coping mechanism for when we feel less cheerful. So now, happily, I know I'm not being ungrateful, but simply storing those precious memories as well as I can."

Milou created the artwork on the cover of this issue

THE COVER

Because we love her botanical artwork so much, we asked Milou Curvers (aka *Mevrouw Knot*, which is Dutch for 'Missus Topknot' because she always wears her hair in a bun) to illustrate the cover for this issue. "I built up the design from separate twigs and leaves, so that I'd be able to move them around. Cover designs tend to be quite fiddly so it's handy if you can make small changes digitally at a later stage. I worked with my favorite Winsor & Newton watercolor paints. I love plants but unfortunately I'm not especially green-thumbed." Milou recently started working full-time with her company Mevrouw Knot. "That was kind of scary, but it gives me so much energy. I'm working on a few great branding and illustration projects, and I'm in the process of putting together my own web shop."

A QUICK CHAT WITH...

More about Valesca on page 139

Valesca van Waveren
Illustrator Valesca van Waveren has been making hand-lettered titles for Flow for a while but she's now also responsible for the illustrated quotes in our regular New Thinkers interview feature. "I love doing hand-lettering for Flow Magazine," she says. "Especially the English editions, because there are more uppercase letters in the headlines, which brings more variety to the image. It always takes a little while to get going. The first headline takes at least six attempts before I'm happy, while the last one takes just one or two tries. With the hand-lettered quotes in the New Thinkers feature, I get to be a bit more playful than with the headlines. I'm not a typographer, but I've had a passion for letters for a long time and they are often part of my illustrations. So Flow asking me to be their 'hand-letterer' feels really quite special!"

PORTRAIT VALESCA ©JONA ROTTING BACKGROUND ILLUSTRATION SUZANNE NUIS

you   you
Y Y Y you a you a y i i
you are y ya
you a @ a a y
Y E E E E a yon y
Y Y E E @ hey
Y Y E E @
E Y E allie
E Y bricca
E a
hey
hey Y Y

v v v v

On the dividers in this issue, you'll find four lifeguard towers on beaches in the US. These towers serve as vantage points for lifeguards, who keep an eye on what's happening on the beach and in the sea.

NOT SHARING

WHO IS IT REALLY FOR, WHEN YOU SHARE PICTURES OF YOUR PARTY, YOUR DANCING CHILDREN OR YOUR PRETTY CUPCAKES ON INSTAGRAM OR FACEBOOK? IS IT FOR YOUR FRIENDS AND FAMILY, OR IS IT REALLY JUST FOR YOU? JOCELYN DE KWANT ASKED HERSELF THIS QUESTION.

'THE ANTICIPATION OF GETTING "LIKES"
PRODUCES A HIGHER LEVEL OF EUPHORIC
HORMONES THAN ACTUALLY GETTING THEM'

My children, aged seven and nine, were sitting in the back of our Volkswagen minivan, singing along and dancing in their seats to the '60s classic *Twist and Shout*. Suddenly I thought, 'Oh, this would be great to share', so I got my phone out and started filming. My son—the youngest—started making even crazier moves, which was no surprise. But the moment my daughter saw I was filming her, something changed in her look and her dancing that startled me a bit. What at first had been a giddy kind of joy with her little brother, became more self-conscious. Her movements became more wooden, even insecure. Just the tiniest bit, but still. She seemed less free. I regretted my decision immediately and stopped filming, but it was already too late. It felt like I had ruined the moment, and it got me thinking: What is it that made me grab my phone at a time like that and to film it? It wasn't for myself or to look back on later—no, my intention very specifically was to share it online. What's more, I was already thinking about the responses it would get. Maybe because I liked it so much myself. Maybe because it had reminded me of my neighbor, who had recently posted a similar video of her children that was so funny I had genuinely laughed out loud. Suddenly I felt deeply disappointed by my own automatic impulse. I could have just kept watching and enjoyed the moment. Why didn't I do that?

"Most people share videos and photos because they really love sharing a nice experience," explains Dutch media psychologist Mischa Coster. "But in the background, all kinds of processes are taking place that also influence your behavior. The human need for social approval, for example. A need for confirmation. Often it's subconscious, but it does play a role."

Coster explains that getting 'likes' generates a small dopamine boost in your body, and that creates a nice feeling. "The remarkable thing is that the *anticipation* of getting 'likes' produces a higher level of euphoric hormones than actually getting them, so that no matter what happens the reality is always a bit disappointing," he says. "And there are more mind games like that going on behind the scenes."

JUST LIKE VEGAS
People are social animals, and social media provides for a social need, Coster says. We don't even think about it very much. But if you engage with these media full on, you can even become dependent on those 'likes' and may need them to feel good about yourself. Then people will do things, purely for the sake of the picture. Young people in particular are vulnerable to this, but adults are not immune either. Cal Newport, an American professor of computer science, does not use social media at all. He is of the opinion that being on social media is more than an innocent pastime. In a TED Talk, Newport says, "...many of the major social media companies hire individuals called attention engineers who borrow principles from Las Vegas casino gambling, among other places, to try to make these products as addictive as possible. That is, the desired use case of these products is that you use it in an addictive fashion, because that maximizes the profit that can be extracted from your attention and data." He also refers to American computer philosophy writer Jaron Lanier, who believes "that these companies offer you shiny treats in exchange for minutes of your attention and bites of your personal data, which can then be packaged up and sold."

It is also called the attention economy: Every tweet, every 'like', every share is worth money. The data is used for marketing purposes or even to obtain political influence. Newport believes we are giving away our private life and our attention to hard-nosed profit models that do not have our best interests at heart. According to him, it's a misunderstanding to think that you need social media, or that you'll be missing out if you don't go on them, or that you're not moving along with the times if you do not use them. "I think I've been more successful professionally because I don't use social media," he says. "Social media is not a fundamental technology [...] it's a source of entertainment, it's an entertainment product. [And] if you look a little bit closer at these technologies, it's not just that they're a source of entertainment, but they're a somewhat unsavory source of entertainment."

DANCE PARTY
This sheds a whole new light on things for me. You can automatically join in with >

'YOU ARE CREATING A TWO-DIMENSIONAL EXPERIENCE
OUT OF A FULL-ON EXPERIENCE THAT YOU COULD BE ENJOYING
RIGHT THERE AND THEN WITH ALL YOUR SENSES'

new things under the guise of moving along with the times, but perhaps 'moving with the times' should also mean being aware of the processes that are going on in the background. Is it really my own choice to decide to post something? Posting something also leads to checking my account to see the responses numerous times, and then responding to them. On average, we look at our phone more than a hundred times a day. How much of that is still free will? Australian philosopher Roman Krznaric said in a recent Flow interview, "We think we are free to make our own choices, but we are being dictated by emails and social media. The art of carpe diem—seizing opportunities and doing things spontaneously—is slipping away. That's why I feel so strongly about the need to take back our freedom."

But do we get our freedom back? And what is that freedom? What do you get back if you no longer spend time and energy sharing things with people who are not there in the moment? First of all, give more attention to the moment itself. People can only focus on one thing at a time. With your camera, you are creating a two-dimensional experience out of a full-on experience that you could be enjoying right then and there with all of your senses; instead of being a participant you become a spectator. That doesn't really make things more fun. Don't get me wrong, I find the videos of dancing people/grandparents/children going viral on social media very interesting. Like the one I saw of a boy at a music festival, who can dance very well. It was lots of fun to watch,

but when the camera panned out, you could see that at least four other friends were also filming the boy. What would have happened if those four people had put their cameras away and also started dancing? Wouldn't that have made the moment even more fun for everyone there? To see the difference, just look at film footage from 1969, of a legendary performance by Tom Jones and Janis Joplin. Joplin makes such a party out of it that the audience can't sit still anymore and they all leap up to dance along. It ends as one big exuberant party. The telling difference between then and now is that nobody had a camera. When you're filming, you can't dance at the same time. You can't even clap.

A THOUSAND EYES ON US
And that's another thing we get back when we stop filming, freedom of movement. We see ourselves more and more frequently through the eyes of others, and only because we're so conscious of the possibility to share the moment. 'How cute do I look when I'm out cycling in the city, with my dog trotting along beside me?' I have seriously asked myself this. Never mind that it's vain, there is another disadvantage: It results in a constant self-awareness. When my father used to pick up his movie camera, that ridiculously big thing that he had to rest on his shoulder, it was hard to miss. My brother and I would break out in exaggerated motions and wave at him (or we just went away); my dad would film for half an hour and then it was done. But now that every moment could end up on Facebook or Instagram as a photo or clip,

we are constantly aware of how we want to look. The presence of a camera simply makes us act differently.

It's related to a psychological phenomenon called 'positive self-presentation bias': when people want to present themselves just a little better than they really are. With close friends and family we're—hopefully—more comfortable with showing our true self, but outside of that inner circle we want to show ourselves to our best advantage. "People have always been that way," Coster says. "It's what we used to do offline, too—when we would see people—but we've never had as many observers as we do now." This positive self-presentation bias is constantly playing a part. That's not only very tiring, it also acts as a block. While before you could act like a fool every now and then with no harm done, today a photo or video clip of you acting that way could stay on the Internet forever.

You can see the magnified effect of this clearly in the most insecure group there is: adolescents. This group is showing more uniformity than ever, and experimenting with clothing is almost a thing of the past. According to Dutch education researcher Marina van der Wal, "Social media has made teenagers dependent on 'likes'. At this age, children are very sensitive to the opinions of others, and those opinions are more visible than ever with all the 'likes', or lack thereof, on social media. As a result, they are much less inclined to take risks."

She's talking about teenagers, but adults are also sensitive to the same issue. >

'IT TAKES DISCIPLINE
NOT TO LET SOCIAL MEDIA
STEAL YOUR TIME'

Alexis Ohanian, American Internet entrepreneur
and co-founder of Reddit

Every artist knows that being preoccupied with the judgment of others is the death knell for creativity and authenticity. By getting rid of the camera, you feel freer to experiment, to make mistakes, to be the odd one out. You can more easily be yourself, including that slouchy back, double chin and bad hairdo.

STAYING IN THE MOMENT

Another thing you get back when you take a more sparing approach to sharing photos: People are still interested in hearing about your vacation. I like to keep my friends and family up to date, but I always feel a bit let down when a friend knows I had a nice vacation because they had already seen the photos online and so there's nothing more to discuss. But when you show someone your vacation pics in person, it's entirely different, because you have a shared moment. And, according to American professor of psychology and author of *Love 2.0*, Barbara Fredrickson, something magical happens in a shared moment. She believes that experiencing a positive moment on your own is good, but a *shared* positive moment becomes much more, because for that brief moment, you both become something bigger than yourself. That is not vague New-Age speak, but is based on sound scientific research. Fredrickson explains that this is because your own positivity evokes a warm and open response from the other person. And vice versa. The shared positivity is reinforced by the attention you give each

other: You smile, and give each other verbal and nonverbal signals of concern, which are powerful and stimulating moments. According to Fredrickson, this doesn't limit itself to interactions between two people, it also works in a group and can even inspire entire social networks or a crowd of people to dance together. Provided we can put those phones and cameras away for a while, and lose ourselves in the moment.

Fredrickson, unlike Newport, is not at all against the use of social media. As long as we realize that it's not a substitute for social encounters in real life. If we let it replace real-life encounters, it would make us unhappy. 'You no doubt try to "stay connected" when physical distance keeps you and your loved ones apart,' she writes. 'You use the phone, email and increasingly texts or Facebook, and it's important to do so. Yet your body, sculpted by the forces of natural selection over millennia, wasn't designed for the abstractions of long-distance love, the XOXs and LOLs. It hungers for more. It hungers for moments of oneness.'

NO SELFIE AT THE CIRCUS

I like to read the funny updates posted by one of the fathers from school, and I can laugh out loud at the photos a colleague makes of her daily trials. It makes me happy to see the photos of distant friends. But now that I'm aware of the processes at play, I want to find a healthy balance. I first notice how my awareness has shifted when I take my children to the circus—their first

one ever. We are sitting in the front row waiting for the show to begin. The lights go out, the spotlights come on and I look at the anticipation in their faces. Instead of giving in to my automatic impulse—'Oh, this is so much fun I want to share it with the world'—I decide to take a deep breath and wrap my arms around them instead. From the corner of my eye I spot the mother next to us taking a selfie with her daughter. The first attempt doesn't work out so the little girl is pulled in for a new picture. And another. And another. Then the mother focuses on her phone posting the photo and writing a caption, the blue light reflecting off her face, her daughter sitting apart from her. My son moves very close to me. I focus on the clowns that are tumbling into the arena and immerse myself in the moment. Better than any circus selfie. ●

WANT TO READ MORE?
----
* 'Love 2.0: Finding Happiness
  and Health in Moments of
  Connection', by Barbara
  Fredrickson

TEXT JOCELYN DE KWANT PHOTOGRAPHY HANKE ARKENBOUT ILLUSTRATION SHUTTERSTOCK

INTERVIEWS **JEANNETTE JONKER** PHOTOGRAPHS **PROVIDED BY THE INTERVIEWEES** HAND-LETTERING **VALESCA VAN WAVEREN** BACKGROUND ILLUSTRATION **SHUTTERSTOCK**

What Are You Up To ?

That's what we asked
three creative entrepreneurs.

CRAFTER
JODI LEVINE
>

Surface designer
JUSTYNA MEDOŃ
>>

INK ARTIST
Katy Smeets
>>>

'I'm working on a children's craft and story book with illustrator Margaret McCartney.'

Finger puppet necklaces, made on a homemade empty toilet roll spool knitter.

In her studio, Jodi has bins of standard craft supplies, as well as 'supermarket' materials.

Jodi Levine

✶ 47 ☛ Crafter, designer and author ⌂ Lives near New York, US, with her husband and two sons ↖ Supermakeit.com

Have you always been a crafter?
Yes, for as long as I can remember I was making things and collecting all sorts of materials. I was totally obsessed with my mom's vintage Betty Crocker cookbooks with all the food-shaped-like-things. My parents encouraged my interests, sending me to art classes and taking me to lots of museums. I studied painting at Rhode Island School of Design and loved trying everything I could while there, like metalsmithing, woodworking and printmaking.

How did crafting became your profession? After my studies, I became a craft editor for *Martha Stewart Living* magazine. It was such an amazing adventure and I learned so much. I eventually became the editorial director of *Martha Stewart Kids* and *Martha Stewart Baby.* After having my two boys and going part-time, I published my first craft book *Candy Aisle Crafts,* with my friend and photographer Amy Gropp Forbes, and then *Paper Goods Projects.* And my blog is all about projects using accessible supermarket materials.

What inspires you? For a long time I collected vintage craft books, booklets and magazines. I still love these old resources, but I also find lots of inspiration by just looking through my bins of materials or going to the supermarket. When I'm feeling stuck, I remember that my best inspiration is the material itself; just playing with it and making stuff. Constraints inspire me too, like an assignment from a client. I don't think I could be in my studio and just make my own work full time.

Can you describe your working space? My studio is in our attic; it has a light-painted wooden floor and white walls and ceiling, so is very bright. I love working up there and feel like I'm floating above the neighborhood. I have lots of supplies and they are sorted into clear plastic bins which makes it easy to find anything. I have a little sink to wash my paintbrushes which feels very luxurious because not all of my workspaces have had that. Our old kitchen island serves as my desk because it's tall and I love to work standing up. >

Toilet tube letters from Jodi's book *Paper Goods Projects.*

'WHEN I'M FEELING STUCK, I REMEMBER MY BEST INSPIRATION IS THE MATERIAL ITSELF'

'I'M INSPIRED BY NATURE, ART HISTORY, GEOMETRY AND SCIENCE'

'Illustrative patterns that tell unique stories: our Flying Castle wall hanging.'

'I love the process of mixing and matching colors to make our wallpapers.'

Justyna Medoń

✖ 35 ☛ Surface pattern designer and printmaker
🏠 Lives in Bristol, UK, with her wife Monika and cat
🔗 Addictedtopatterns.uk

Can you tell us about your work?
I studied Surface Design at University of the Arts London in the UK, and found my passion for printmaking, wallpapers and textiles. After graduating, I moved to my native Poland for a few years and co-founded Red Poppy studio in Warsaw. In 2015, my wife Monika and I moved to Bristol, UK, and we founded Addicted to Patterns. I design one collection each year, which includes new patterns and color variations for existing designs. I'm currently preparing our new wall hangings collection and am getting ready for some exhibitions.

What inspires you? I'm inspired by nature, art history, geometry and science. And also the accidental marks created in the printmaking process.

What is your specialty? The combination of organic and geometric motifs. Whenever I think about patterns, I try to merge them together. I love printing on a large scale, which is why wall hangings are one of my favorite surfaces to cover. They give you space to work with a repeating pattern or allow you to drift and create large-scale illustrative murals.

How does the collaboration with Monika work? Monika has her own studio space where she does digital design, writing and calligraphy. When I work on design ideas I share them with her and we always hang a proof print in our bedroom, so when we wake up we can see if we like it or if changes need to be made. I rely on Monika's opinion and I value it. Sometimes it's hard to take criticism, but it motivates me to rework things and find different angles.

What are your little pleasures in life? We celebrate every breakfast, and love having coffee together. I would say that we really care about how we start our day. Little pleasures include jumping on a train or bus, with a sleeping bag, and just going somewhere for 24 hours; taking long walks and discovering new places around Bristol; spending time in the garden; reading; and taking care of our plants. >

'My studio is my little sanctuary of peace and quiet.'

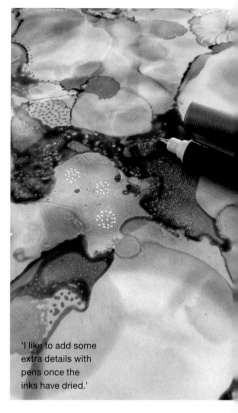

'I like to add some extra details with pens once the inks have dried.'

Katy Smeets

✖ 37 ☛ Ink Artist ♟ Lives in Adelaide, Australia, with her husband and two sons ↖ Katyjdesigns.etsy.com

When did you start painting? After working as a graphic designer for over ten years, I was unexpectedly made redundant while on maternity leave after the birth of my second son. I decided to embrace this time with my young family and really re-evaluated what I wanted in a creative job. I wanted to explore my creativity in new ways that didn't always involve using a computer.

What is it about ink you like so much? I fell in love with it from the first time that I used it. I was instantly addicted to the inks' vibrancy and organic flow. The dyes that are in alcohol inks give them an unpredictable behavior, which can be challenging, but also surprising and exciting. As a sufferer of anxiety, I find the process of painting with inks very relaxing and it allows me to completely switch off from the outside world and immerse myself in my painting.

What kind of materials do you use? Alcohol inks and rubbing alcohol on special coated paper called Yupo Paper. I rarely use a paintbrush; instead I push

and guide the inks to let them pool, bloom and dry in order to get the effects I'm looking for. I sometimes like to add some extra detail with Posca pens.

How would you describe your style? My paintings are usually abstract and a celebration of the patterns, textures and colors found in the natural world. I usually have an idea of the colors I would like to work with but the rest I leave up to the inks to work their magic. I've recently explored new ways to use my paintings, such as incorporating them into animals and people.

What do you do on a day off? I love heading to the beach with my husband and boys. We are so lucky to be living in Adelaide where we are spoiled with gorgeous beaches. There's just something about walking along the beach that clears my head and relaxes me, even in winter. We also like to go to the National Park to spot koalas and kangaroos. I love wandering around local art and craft markets or meet up with friends for a coffee. ●

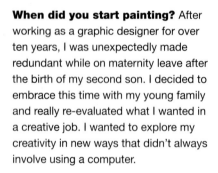

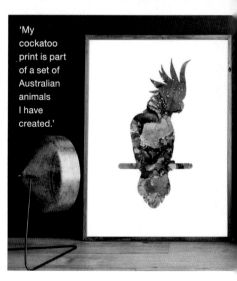

'My cockatoo print is part of a set of Australian animals I have created.'

'I RARELY USE A PAINTBRUSH; INSTEAD I PUSH AND GUIDE THE INKS TO GET THE EFFECTS I'M LOOKING FOR'

Never miss an issue

SUBSCRIBE TO FLOW

JOIN FLOW ANYWHERE IN THE WORLD

With our international subscription service, you can get Flow Magazine delivered to you anywhere in the world, guaranteed within seven days of it being published. We offer a six- or three-issue subscription.

———————————

ABOUT FLOW

Flow is a magazine that takes its time. It's about doing things differently, making new choices and enjoying life's little pleasures. About positive psychology, mindfulness, creativity and the beauty of imperfection. We love illustrations and in each issue you'll find a gift made from our much-loved material: paper.

———————————

GO TO FLOWMAGAZINE.COM/SUBSCRIPTION FOR PRICES AND FURTHER DETAILS.

PHOTOGRAPHY @HANKE ARKENBOUT   BACKGROUND IMAGE SHUTTERSTOCK

Lemonade
Is All Grown Up Now

NEITHER ACHINGLY SWEET NOR ALARMINGLY
GREEN, THE LEMONADES OF TODAY HAVE
EXCITING NEW FLAVORS AND ARE MADE FROM
PURE, NATURAL INGREDIENTS.

When we were children and went to visit our Grandma, two glasses were always standing ready on the granite kitchen counter for my brother and me. Usually it was the classic Dutch lemonade known as Ranja: vividly orange in color and with a sickly-sweet flavor. Sometimes she bought grenadine. And when she bought the green stuff, we were really happy. The flavor didn't matter—it was that crazy green hue that we just totally loved.

We never could have dreamed back then that syrup drinks would be making a big comeback 40 years later. Or that cool tattooed hipsters would be the ones putting this old-fashioned children's drink back on the map. Its resurgence is strong. First the syrups, lemonades and alternative soft drinks started appearing on food trucks and at music festivals, and now dozens of syrups and ready-made lemonades are available in local supermarkets. Known by many different names—lemonade, syrup, cordial or squash—they are being sold in small or big bottles, in pretty shapes and with beautiful labels. And now that just about every department store and supermarket has a house-brand syrup or lemonade (complete with swingtop bottle and retro label) in its range, it's pretty clear that the trend has transcended the hipster hype.

MAKE YOUR OWN

* Heat a cup of water and a cup of sugar in a pan over a low heat and stir until the sugar has dissolved.

* Mix the syrup together with a cup of freshly-squeezed lemon juice in a large jug. Stir well and allow to cool. Fill the rest of the jug with (carbonated) water and, if you like, ice cubes. Serve with mint and a slice of lemon.

* You can make endless variations with this basic recipe. For example, you can add pureed fruit, such as strawberries, melons, mangoes, berries, nectarines, peaches or raspberries.

PULLING RECIPES FROM THE ARCHIVES

German brand Bionade was perhaps the very first new-style lemonade to make it big. The makers started small, without any budget for marketing or advertising, and despite this, their lemonade quickly became a very popular underground hit. In 2002, two million bottles were sold, and in 2007 sales hit about two hundred million. Bionade has been important for the burgeoning lemonade trend, says Paul Löhndorf, one of the founders of the German lemonade brand Proviant. Proviant now employs thirty people and distributes to nine countries: it has also become much bigger than Löhndorf ever could have imagined. It was never his intention to be a lemonade producer. He was planning to start a café with two friends on the university campus in Berlin, but the location they had set their sights on fell through. They decided to sell the drinks that they had been inventing for the café—smoothies and lemonades—to festivals instead. And that took off like a rocket. First restaurants became their clients, then a large German organic supermarket chain >

'It fits in with what we find important at the moment... We are looking for the authentic flavors of pure and local products, made with passion. In other words: a world apart from the soft drink industry'

asked if they could add Proviant to their product offering. "Time after time, we would move to a larger building, but grow too big for it," Löhndorf says. "I could also see the success all around me; in the restaurant business it used to be all about the food, but now you see elaborate drinks menus with specialty beers and artisanal lemonades everywhere."

The success of Dutch brand Saru Soda was just as unexpected. A few years ago, Leslie Dronkers was still working at a market every Saturday with his own organic specialties: homemade elderflower syrup, rillettes, pâté and olives. Now he and his partner have a syrup factory, with almost twenty different kinds rolling off the production belt, from classic flavors such as berries and blood orange, to novel combinations like pine/agave or lemongrass/ginger. "We started small, and sold our beverages to alternative cafés and cocktail bars," Dronkers says, "but the business just keeps on growing." All the syrups are made from fresh products. "Hard ingredients" Dronkers calls them. "Whole pallets of elderflower, Darjeeling tea, rhubarb, rose petals, spices, you name it, are processed in our factory. Some ingredients—and therefore the syrups themselves—are seasonal, such as the rhubarb, which really is a cold-season crop, because you can't make tasty syrup out of greenhouse rhubarb." Dronkers scoped the Internet and also went digging through old pharmacy archives, and found several obscure recipes. That's how he came across a cola recipe from 1886 which they tried out. "We had to make a lot of changes," he says. "For example, the original drink turned out to be very sweet. We were experimenting for two-and-a-half years before we ended up with the perfect recipe. Each and every change, no matter how small, has an effect on the taste: how you roast the spices, for example, even the order in which you add the ingredients."

THE TASTE OF A PINE FOREST

Food designer Marielle Bordewijk is not surprised that syrups and lemonade have turned into such a success story. "It fits in with what we find important at the moment: things that are homemade and traditional," she says. "We are looking for the authentic flavors of pure and local products, made with passion. In other words: a world apart from the soft drink industry. Also, with the syrups you can dose the flavor yourself so you have control over how sweet you want your drink to be. And syrup is more sustainable because it is distributed in its concentrated form. That makes a huge difference in weight on the road, which makes transportation more environmentally friendly. Those are three important factors that are giving old-fashioned syrup a new lease on life. Another interesting thing is that lemonade is easy to make in small batches, so restaurants can use them to raise their own profile."

Well-known brands from the past have also been dusted off, reintroduced or given a new lease of life with a range of 'hip' flavors, like SodaStream (a popular accessory in many a '70s or '80s kitchen), Exota (a brand that had been declared bankrupt in the '70s), or Ranja (which for most Dutch people is just a synonym for the word 'lemonade'). A few young entrepreneurs who are in the business of breathing new life into old home-grown brands, purchased the Ranja brand name. Their updated version has an old-school label and the Ranja of now looks a lot lighter in color, because the punchy orange, crimson red and poisonous green hues of the '80s are just unacceptable with today's aesthetics.

Consumers want everything to be natural, says Rachael Reeder Orisé of French brand Rième Boissons, (most famous for their La Mortuacienne syrup), which has been owned by her family for almost a hundred years. They too have modified the food dyes they use, while in other respects the recipes have remained >

@jes_wlf

@proviantberlin

@fentimansltd

@bionade

@strawberrybumblebee

@hosgreta

@proviantberlin

@spreegold.freshfoodanddrinks

@paulakusti

@s_m_ni

@proviantberlin

@jemrenee9

the same. "La Mortuacienne started in 1921 with three flavors: lemon, grenadine and mint," Reeder Orisé says. "We now have 38 flavors—each generation adds some new flavors, and sometimes one or two disappear. But the classics of the first hour are still our bestsellers. And pine forest is very popular; it is typical of this region with its numerous pine trees. People here love it."

In France, syrup is deeply embedded in the culture, but it still has experienced fluctuations in popularity. At the beginning of the 20th century, it was very popular in the French hospitality industry, says Reeder Orisé. "It was drunk in cafés as a non-alcoholic refreshment, or mixed with red or white wine," she says. "After the Second World War, for a long period syrups were considered something for children, and since the 1990s the drink has been making a comeback." La Mortuacienne is benefiting from the international lemonade hype. For example, in London the swingtop bottles stand side by side with chic foods in department store Harrods' delicatessen. And in Germany it is also seen as an exclusive beverage, priced more expensively than most other syrups and lemonades. "People are willing to pay more for it there, while in France it's still an everyday drink that you can simply buy in the supermarkets."

FUTURE PROOF
The Germans in particular appear to be keen to take on the big soft drinks brands. "There was fritz-kola, for example, which a group of friends in Hamburg started producing in 2003, with only €7,000 in startup capital, to create an alternative to the big well-known colas," says trend researcher Silvia Naber. The trend is now firmly established and, according to Bordewijk, we

haven't seen the last of lemonade for a while yet. "We've become fed up with soft drinks, which are oversaturated with sugar. People want to decide for themselves how sweet they'll have their drinks. That also fits in with today's health trends. Lemonade is all grown up now. We're going to be seeing more new brands and quirky flavors: with herbs or spices, on the basis of fermented fruit or from vegetables like beets or cucumber. But there is also a lot of competition. Flavored waters—water flavored with some mint, ginger or lemon—in particular are doing well and they are completely calorie-free."

A trend usually lasts about ten years and we are now at its peak, Naber says. "On café terraces you can see lemonade now competing with alcoholic beverages, because of the exciting flavor combinations," she says. "Natural selection will thin them out in the long run and a only few of the new brands will keep their place on our store's shelves. Other lemonades or syrups, for example the ones with the far-out flavors, will disappear. But for the time being, the lemonade wave is riding high." ●

WANT TO READ MORE?
....
✳ 'Pop, Bubble & Fizz', by Tove Nilsson
....

TEXT **ANNEKE BOTS** PHOTOGRAPHY ©**TANA TEEL/STOCKSY UNITED** (OPENING IMAGE) ILLUSTRATIONS **DEBORAH VAN DER SCHAAF**

AVAILABLE ONLINE FROM NOVEMBER 13, 2018

FLOW BOOK FOR PAPER LOVERS 6

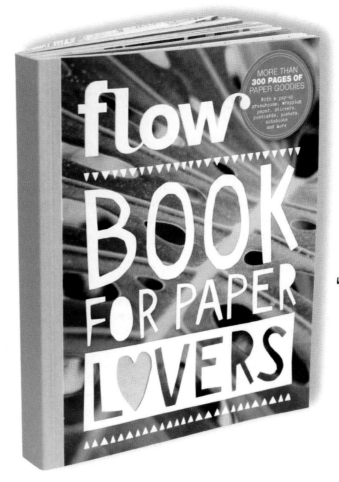

Find out more about what's inside this year's edition on page 132.

This annual bestseller contains no less than 300 pages of paper goodies and hardly any text. Once again, we collaborated with a large team of illustrators from all around the world who are just as crazy about paper as we are. For the sixth edition, we created a celebration of nature, of its flowers, plants, animals and forests.

———————————

This book contains: Labels ✳ Stickers ✳ Mini cards ✳ Postcards ✳ Envelopes ✳ Writing paper ✳ A Garland ✳ A Pop-up Greenhouse and Plants ✳ Posters ✳ Wrapping Paper ✳ A Booklet ✳ A Birthday Calendar ✳ And More

THE FLOW BOOK FOR PAPER LOVERS 6 IS AVAILABLE ONLINE FROM NOVEMBER 13, 2018, AND COSTS €21.95. ORDER YOUR COPY AT FLOWMAGAZINE.COM/BFPL6

PHOTOGRAPHY **WIKE ZIJLSTRA** BACKGROUND IMAGE AND ILLUSTRATION **SHUTTERSTOCK**

FLOW 2019 WALL CALENDAR

Ring binding for easy use

With stickers and postcards

The My Perfectly Imperfect Life 2019 Wall Calendar (30 x 30 cm / 11.8 x 11.8 inch) celebrates slowing down, making mistakes, keeping an open mind, embracing imperfection, and finding beauty everywhere you look. Each month is filled with colorful artwork by illustrator Karen Weening, as well as tips on how to let go of daily stress, change your perspective, and step out of your comfort zone. Also included are ideas for Doing Nothing Plans, twelve full-color illustrated postcards and dozens of stickers.

THE MY PERFECTLY IMPERFECT LIFE 2019 WALL CALENDAR COSTS €15.99. IT IS AVAILABLE TO ORDER FROM THE FLOW WEB SHOP (WHILE STOCKS LAST), AND IN BOOKSTORES ACROSS THE US. FLOWMAGAZINE.COM/SHOP

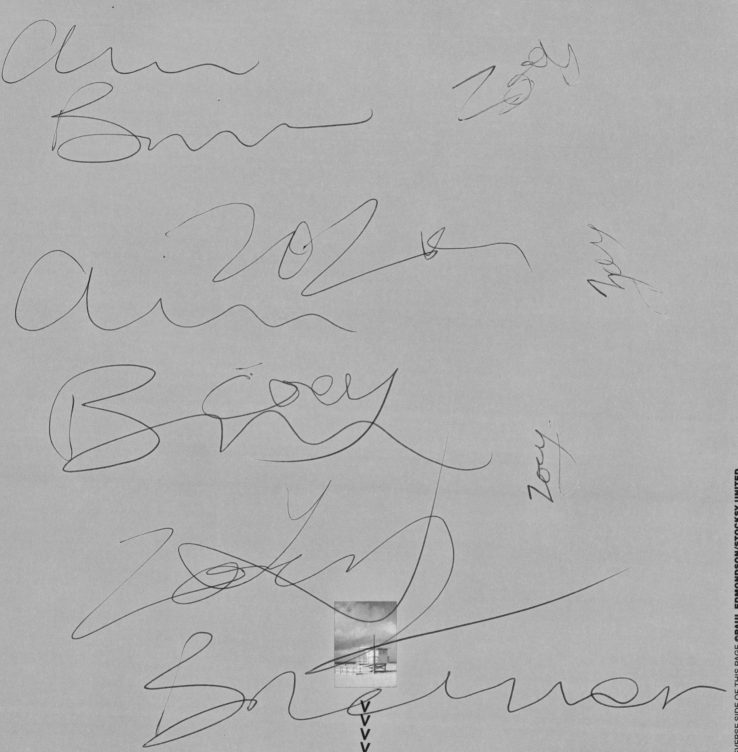

The most famous lifeguard tower in the world is probably the one from the
American TV series *Baywatch* (which was broadcast from 1989 to 2001).
The series revolved around a group of lifeguards on Santa
Monica beach in California, US. Apart from storylines about hazardous
rescue missions, averting shark attacks and searching for lost children, the
series focused on the lives and loves of the lifeguard community.

COLETTE (1873-1954)
French novelist

WHAT A WONDERFUL LIFE I'VE HAD!

I only wish I'd realized it sooner

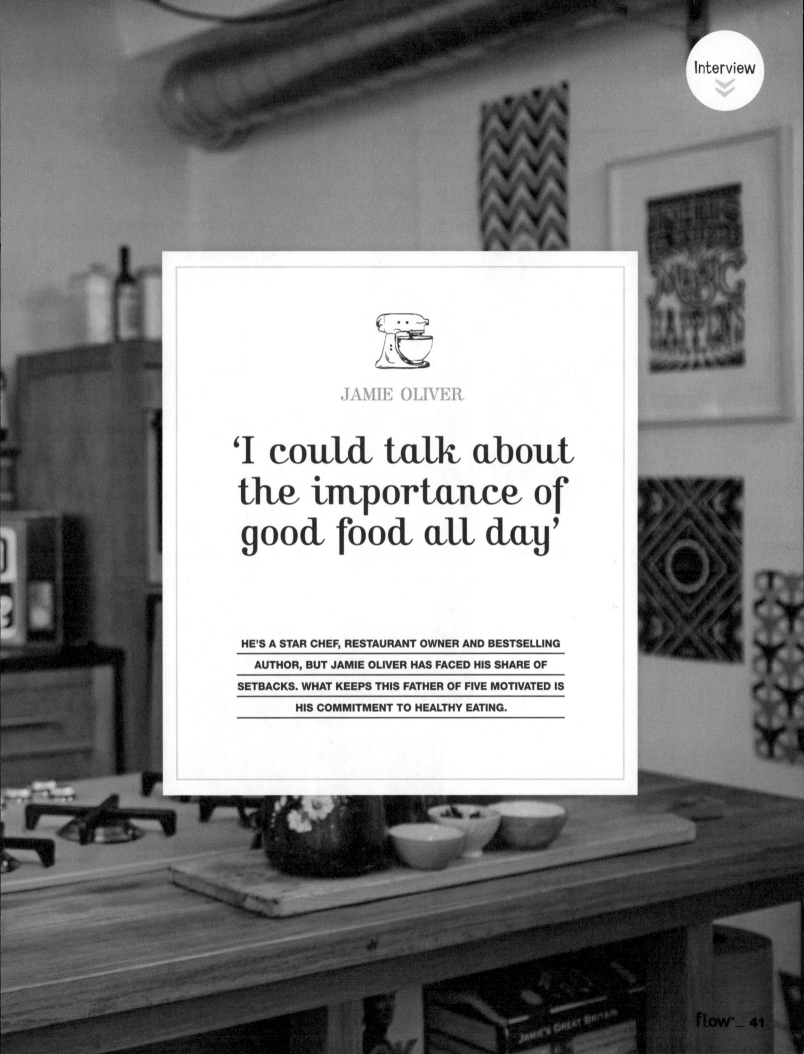

JAMIE OLIVER

'I could talk about the importance of good food all day'

HE'S A STAR CHEF, RESTAURANT OWNER AND BESTSELLING
AUTHOR, BUT JAMIE OLIVER HAS FACED HIS SHARE OF
SETBACKS. WHAT KEEPS THIS FATHER OF FIVE MOTIVATED IS
HIS COMMITMENT TO HEALTHY EATING.

My younger sister and me with
our grandmother

I met my
wife Jools
when I was
17; this photo
is from 2001

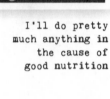

I'll do pretty
much anything in
the cause of
good nutrition

I used to play in the sandpit
with Jimmy Doherty (right);
now we have the TV show 'Jamie
and Jimmy's Food Fight Club'

My mates from
when I was a kid
keep my feet on
the ground today

NAME: James Trevor Oliver MBE
BORN: 1975
OCCUPATION: Chef & restaurateur.
Jamie achieved international
fame with his TV show 'The
Naked Chef' in 1999. He opened
his first restaurant, Fifteen,
in London, UK, in 2002, offering
opportunities for socially
disadvantaged young people
to train for careers in the
restaurant business. He also
started promoting healthy food
in UK schools, such as the 2005
Feed Me Better campaign. There
are now branches of his various
restaurants in more than twenty
countries. Jamie is the author
of 24 cookbooks, the most recent
being 'Jamie Cooks Italy'.

What a gift—
with my sister
at Christmas

I didn't like
school, I was a
lousy pupil

PAST

'BY AGE FIVE, I WAS ALREADY HELPING OUT IN MY PARENTS' PUB...

I SOON UNDERSTOOD: IF YOU WANT TO GET ANYWHERE,

YOU HAVE TO ROLL UP YOUR SLEEVES AND GET ON WITH IT'

I grew up a real country boy in Clavering, in the county of Essex, about 18 miles from Cambridge. By age five, I was already helping out in my parents' pub The Cricketers, washing glasses and chopping veg for £1 an hour. I was really good with the knife even back then, and to be honest, I cooked up some really good grub, even as a kid. But my parents taught me something else really important: a great work ethic and how to treat others with respect and friendliness, and how to stay polite even when you're stressed and your feet are killing you. I sometimes wish my own kids could help their grandparents out now and again, and learn all that. Back then I soon understood: if you want to get anywhere, you have to roll up your sleeves and get on with it.

My parents were working class; I have no idea why all these people I met later with my food show *The Naked Chef* on TV thought I was some privileged rich kid who went to a private school. Actually I was a chubby, thick kid who was so bad at school I needed extra lessons for the simplest things.

I found out for the first time that you can do magic with food when I was young. I went into the woods for a picnic with some friends and gave one of them his first ever smoked salmon sandwich, which I'd squeezed some slices of lemon over. I'll never forget the look on his face when that combination of salty, smoky, soft bread and lemon hit his tongue. That was a real 'aha!' moment—for him, as well as for me. I've given each of my children exactly the same sandwich at one time or another. It's a really special occasion, every time.

I met my wife Jools—her name's actually Juliette—when I was 17. We've been together ever since. I'm a romantic guy: When Jools went to Tokyo for three months once for a job, I sent her a love letter every day. She kept them all. After secondary school, I left Essex and went to Westminster College, to study catering. Jools worked as a waitress. I was as poor as a church mouse; at the end of the month, I'd hardly have £100 left, and without Jools' tips things would have been really grim. **We both had a clear idea of our future: I wanted to spend five years cooking in different restaurants in London, then we'd open a good pub back home and live above it with our family.** Jools already wanted a lot of children back then. I thought she meant like two; turns out I was wrong. We're now up to five children. Living above the pub like that could have been enough for us. In fact, I think Jools would have liked a more modest life. At least, she never pushed me career-wise.

My first job was in the Neal Street Restaurant, and I worked under Italian chef Gennaro Contaldo. I'm still great friends with him today; we just did my new Italy cookbook together. And one of my colleagues there was Tim Mälzer. Later I went on to work in the River Café. One day, a BBC team was shooting a program there about my bosses, Rose Gray and Ruth Rogers. And I was in it. Afterward, the producer asked me if I'd be interested in having my own show. That's how I ended up being the star of *The Naked Chef*, in 1999. That show really took off, it was completely incredible what happened. Within six weeks, I had a few million in my bank account. Only thing was, the BBC wanted it to look like I was single. So when they were filming at our place, Jools had to stay in the bedroom. We got married the following year, in the summer of 2000, in All Saints Church in Rickling Green in Essex. Jools in a stunning long white dress, me in a light blue suit by Paul Smith and snakeskin shoes.

My cookery show ran for three years. Alongside that, I wrote a few cookbooks and got some advertising contracts. But **I was naive, precocious, and had a lot of money. Three things that are a very dangerous combination.** >

PRESENT

**'I'VE NEVER BEEN A BUSINESSMAN; TODAY, I STILL MAKE
A LOT OF DECISIONS ON THE BASIS OF TRIAL AND ERROR,
BUT I'VE ALWAYS BEEN ABLE TO MOTIVATE PEOPLE'**

Following my breakthrough with *The Naked Chef*, I suddenly had all these opportunities. All the TV stations wanted me. I was sleeping three-and-a-half hours a night at most—the speed of this success was incredible. I could have retired to a country estate as a rich man at 26. But I wanted to grow as an entrepreneur. Maybe because I wanted to show myself and everyone else that I was good for something, having done so miserably at school. It was then I got the idea for my first restaurant, Fifteen. I wanted to use it to train 30 unemployed young people as chefs. I put all my money into the project—a lot of people warned me against it, especially my father. I've never been a businessman; today I still make a lot of decisions on the basis of trial and error. But I've always been able to motivate people. So I ended up opening Fifteen in 2002.

By working with these young people—whom we pretty much picked up off the streets—**I came to understand how disadvantaged people feel, what it means not to have any positive examples. My work got more political. I got more and more interested in how children and young people are growing up in England**, started fighting against fast food, collected signatures for a campaign for healthier nutrition in schools, which finally led the Labour government to make £280 million available for a project to support school canteens. At the same time, I was making about six cookery shows a year, writing books, setting up my own TV production company and opening restaurants in different countries all over the world. At a certain point, I realized I was destroying my health. I could almost see the burnout coming: I had bad blood circulation, wasn't getting enough sleep. I was getting close to the edge. So I started eating more healthily, cut out salt and drank no alcohol after 10 p.m. I also went through a fitness program and started getting more sleep. During this period, I realized how precious your health is.

Business didn't always go smoothly. Despite all the success, I must have lost so many millions. I would say 40 percent of my projects didn't make it in the end. In a lot of cases, the timing was bad; some just didn't work. I also got my fingers burned with some 'buddy projects', where I got friends into various different positions. I've now learned that it doesn't pay to mix your business and private life. Then came the whole story about me supposedly being bankrupt. The press wrote that I was the equivalent of €53 million in debt, and that I couldn't pay my rent, suppliers and staff. Most of the problems were in the British restaurants, and it's true that twelve of these had to close.

That was the hardest time of my life. Maybe I trusted a few people a bit too much. I spent a lot of time thinking. I also shed a few tears into my pillow. But pain can be a great teacher, so in that way it was a very useful time for me. You just have to find a way to get through it. **I meditated a lot. In my case, this means cooking really well, with extreme concentration. It's a form of attentiveness that I find incredibly liberating.** I like to listen to melancholy music while I'm doing it; it really helps me to think. And of course my personality helps too: I'm a very optimistic person, my glass is always half full.

I never talk to Jools about business. I spar enough with my team about the job. And Jools really isn't interested. She always wanted to be a good mother, and in that respect she's got a fantastic career. She has a fulfilled life, she lives her role. When I get home in the evening and close the door behind me, home is my world. We talk about the kids' school, homework, how we are bringing them up. How we can be good parents, what we could do better. Jools and I think very similarly about this. We certainly don't spoil them: the younger kids inherit stuff from the older ones, we go on 'staycations' in Norfolk or Cornwall. All really normal. My children aren't always thinking, 'Wow, what a great dad I've got'. I'm mostly an embarrassment to them. If I want to take them somewhere, they say, "Do you have to? Can't mom do it?" >

A PR tour
in Tim
Mälzer's
Bullerei
in Hamburg
in 2011

Soon after the birth
of River Rocket

'The
Naked
Chef'
in 2001

2013, with
my German
colleagues
Tim Raue
(left) and
Tim Mälzer
(right) in
Berlin

I had to learn
to relax

Royal handshake: Rick Stein
(second left) and I won the 2012
Cook for the Queen competition

With my second youngest son,
Buddy Bear Maurice

My latest
cookbook,
'Jamie Cooks
Italy'

FUTURE

'I AM EXCITED WHEN I THINK ABOUT THE FUTURE, BUT I'M ALSO A LITTLE CONCERNED. I REALLY HOPE THAT MY VISION BECOMES REALITY'

I'm actually really happy; I have the right balance in my life. I've written 24 cookbooks on various aspects of cooking, and they're being sold in 120 countries. I also have a business that employs more than 5,000 people, and many successful restaurants, as well as a name that is a brand. Nevertheless, it's not always easy being Jamie Oliver. Every time I meet someone, they've already got an opinion about me. Everyone thinks they already know me. I can't just nip to the supermarket—someone always wants to talk to me. And people are always watching me: What's he buying, what is he going to do next? They're all nice people, but the twenty minutes I was planning to be away soon turns into two hours. But on the other hand, this fame is what gives me the platform to achieve what I want to achieve.

I am really passionate about improving food in schools, and I am also campaigning to make the food in supermarkets better and healthier. In recent years, I have often noticed that, although I'm a good speaker, I sometimes don't have the in-depth background knowledge, and this is a weak point that makes me vulnerable in discussions. For this reason, **I've gone back to school and I'm doing a master's degree in nutritional science. I'm learning to analyze statistics and join in the more scientific discussions.** This means I am able to evaluate the public health system and its faults

better than before. And suddenly the authorities are taking me more seriously. Whereas they used to see me as some kind of pop star, now they see my message, and respect me more. I'm automatically following a different path. It's like switching from pop music to classical. From entertainment to serious culture. And it's probably the same as with a lot of things: You first have to learn the language of the people you are talking to. This is the only way to be understood, and to understand the others. **I still feel insecure when I have to deal with important people from the government. Unfortunately, it's not always just about the issues: some people like you, and others just don't.**

But my message hasn't changed through all this: if I could, I'd spend all day talking about how important good, nutritious food is. For children and young people, but also for adults. I'm not knocking chips; I just don't understand when people have to eat them every single day. So many young people are overweight. It doesn't have to be like this. I'm really proud of what we've achieved so far, and it's not just me. Also our campaign to stop under-16s drinking energy drinks full of sugar and caffeine. One big retail chain has now banned the sale of these to young people. In the months ahead, we'll be really stepping up the fight for our goals; we want to achieve more. I am

noticing that I do have influence. I can change things locally, but also at national level—make the world a slightly better place. I've really found my role. Everyone needs an aim in life, I think. Something you believe in, something to fight for. **Whether I've done the right thing in life, at some point I'll have to account for it, to myself. I want to be able to say, on my deathbed, 'I did some good'. That would be a good ending.**

What about twenty years from now? I'll have wrinkles and be very, very tired. But hopefully things will be a lot better for British children, as far as nutrition is concerned. And I'll still be celebrating good food. I am excited when I think about the future. But I'm also a little concerned. I really hope that my vision becomes reality, and not just a great dream.

I am done with one thing, though, I think: family planning. After the birth of our fifth child, River Rocket—our daughters Daisy and Poppy cut the umbilical cord by the way—I was pretty wiped out. Jools says never say never, but there's no more room in my car now. If we had another kid we'd have to get a minibus. And to be brutally honest, I hate buses. ●

TEXT **SILKE PFERSDORF** PHOTOGRAPHY **CAMERA PRESS/PICTURE PRESS** (OPENING PHOTO), **REDUX/LAIF, GAMMA-RAPHO/LAIF, ALLPIX/LAIF, DAVID LOFTUS** (PORTRAITS), **SAM ROBINSON** (FAMILY PORTRAIT), **PRIVATE** ILLUSTRATIONS **SHUTTERSTOCK**

READING
retreat

A weekend in a house with other readers,
a huge pile of books and a reading coach.
Flow editor Marije van der Haar-Peters
decided to give it a try.

When our group is asked, 'What do you really want to do?', the word that rises straight to the surface is 'Read'. I am sitting in an arthouse cinema, about to watch the documentary *A Mindful Choice*, but first we listen to a brief introduction from an Ishaya monk. The next question the group is asked is, 'Are you living according to what you want most? And what can you do to make more room for this in your life?' In the days that follow, I occasionally revisit these last two questions. Sure, I read quite a lot (around 25 to 30 books a year), but not as much as I would like. And when I do decide to read a book, it's hard to always stay focused on it for long periods of time. Work, deadlines, to-do lists, Netflix and my telephone (that is never more than arm's length away) distract me. These are all things that I apparently subconsciously prioritize even though I can't imagine anything better than allowing myself to be swept away by the words on a page, to worlds near or far, to other lives. I feel that reading enriches me as a person, perhaps even makes me wiser. Ideas or opinions that are firmly rooted in my head are questioned or more focused. Even the most unsympathetic main character can appear to have a vulnerable side, struggling with large or small issues. Sometimes my eyes fill with tears when I read a beautiful sentence, but it's not just the beauty of the language that interests me. Nearly every book I read contains a short, simple sentence that will suddenly resonate with me, that puts into words something that lies dormant somewhere. A sentence that makes me think, 'Yes! That's exactly how that feels'.

THREE DAYS OF READING

I decide to sign up for a reading retreat. Cécile Wilbers is a literature coach, and gives people personalized reading tips based on what suits them and what they're interested in at this point in their lives. She got the idea for her weekend retreats after having heard so often that people don't have enough time to really read all the wonderful books she recommends. So here I am, on a Friday afternoon, driving to a former game warden's house (picture a little white house with a thatched roof, fireplace,

finish something or be somewhere. But the peace and quiet required to read is something I will be recreating when I get home.

As the other six participants slowly arrive in the hours that follow, I realize our motivations for being here don't differ all that much. None of us get around to reading as much as we would like to, and we are all looking forward to a weekend for ourselves, no full schedules and no distractions. Before I came here, I thought it might be awkward to suddenly share a living room with complete

'NEARLY EVERY BOOK I READ CONTAINS A SHORT, SIMPLE SENTENCE THAT WILL SUDDENLY RESONATE WITH ME'

floral wallpaper and large rustic kitchen) at an estate in a rural part of the country. I am surrounded by walnut trees, fields, farmland and even a pumpkin patch, as far as the eye can see. The view lends itself well for musing about the book between reading sessions. The aromas of soup and pie permeate the interior, and a beautiful little notebook and pencil have been laid out on my bed. This relaxed, informal, almost carefree vibe remains throughout the weekend; no mandatory schedule, you are welcome to eat breakfast when you feel like it or even crawl back into bed with your book. There are no responsibilities when it comes to meals and the corresponding chores. It takes some getting used to in the beginning, suddenly not having to

strangers, but this fear soon goes. We exchange book recommendations now and then, but then we return to our books and the only sound I hear is the turning of pages. There is something cozy about reading with other people and it has a connecting effect, even if you're all reading different books.

FINALE

This weekend, I am starting *The End of Loneliness* by Benedict Wells, a book that has come highly recommended by a few people, and I can already tell that these recommendations are completely justified. It is a beautiful story about a boy named Jules and his brother and sister, who lose their parents at a young age and go from idyllic family to living >

Cécile's recent favorite novels: 'Aquarium' by David Vann, 'Bird Cottage' by Eva Meijer and 'The Underground Railroad' by Colson Whitehead **flow**_ 49

'READING ISN'T JUST LAZING AROUND; READING IS ABOUT NOURISHING AND INSPIRING OURSELVES. MAKE IT A PRIORITY AND ALLOW YOURSELF THIS WONDERFUL EXPERIENCE'

at a boarding school. From that moment on, they have to learn to manage on their own for the most part, but at the same time their lives remain connected throughout the entire book. This includes the normal drama that goes on between siblings, yet also always with that spark of solidarity. It is about how we have the feeling that our lives aren't real, that we are only half alive until our parents come home. It's also about how we pick ourselves back up again and ultimately shape ourselves to our circumstances, even when it comes to love.

You would think that with a great story like this you just open the book and away you go, losing yourself in it. After reading a few lines however,

I find myself lost in random snippets of thought, and can't even remember what these were about. This is a familiar phenomenon for Wilbers. "In the beginning, it's hard to clear your head enough to start reading and sometimes you feel resistance rising up," she says. "Just make sure that you keep at it for the first six to ten minutes, at which point you'll be absorbed by the story."

The next day, during the one-on-one sessions we all have with Wilbers, we return to this issue. As we walk, I talk about how I sometimes feel so lazy every time I miss the opportunity to read or when I only manage to read half a page in an entire evening. Sometimes it seems like I can't concentrate on anything,

particularly after a busy day at work, so my evenings feel so fragmented. Wilbers recommends consciously making room in my schedule for reading. "It helps to see reading as something you want to make time for," she says. "We often put demands on ourselves to do and finish everything first, and then we 'are allowed' to grab a book in the time remaining. But reading isn't just lazing around; reading is about nourishing and inspiring ourselves. Make it a priority and allow yourself this wonderful experience."

I realize that I have subconsciously started seeing reading as a sort of 'finale' in my life. And because there is typically no room left for what I really want to do, it gnaws at me. As business psychologist Tony Crabbe (author of the book, *Busy: How to Thrive in a World of Too Much*) explains in a newspaper article, 'People say, "As soon as I have more time, I'm going to do this and that". This is never going to happen when you take this approach and this is why you need to get rid of your to-do list. Do you ever put the things that are really important to you on this list? I don't have "spend time with my children" or "write a second book" on my to-do list. If a list like this is the manual, by definition, you are not doing what is most important to you'.

ENERGY SOURCE

Wilbers ties every reading retreat to a book that has made a deep impression on her. She and Mariana, who is responsible for the catering, also gear all the food and music to this 'theme'. This weekend, the book is *The Heart is a Lonely Hunter* by Carson McCullers, an

TIPS FOR A READING DIP

"Find a book that really suits you or ask someone who reads a lot for recommendations," says literature coach Cécile Wilbers. "Go to bed half an hour earlier or stay in bed longer in the morning with a book. Don't be afraid to set it aside if you are not getting enough out of it." The barrier is lower with a shorter book, such as 'Silk' by Alessandro Baricco, 'Of Mice and Men' by John Steinbeck, or 'The List of My Desires' by Grégoire Delacourt.

unconventional woman from the deep South of the US who was very critical of the racism and poverty that dominated this region. During the literary dinner on Saturday evening, Wilbers talks more about McCullers' life, and reads the first chapter aloud between courses. We also listen to music by Suzanne Vega, who admired McCullers from a young age and recorded an album as a tribute to her work and life. As we are served the most delicious dishes (with a nip of whiskey to finish them off), I realize again how this nourishes me, talking about books with others and getting recommendations for books we might have not discovered on our own. I decide to seek out a book group to join and listen to writers more often, purely because it makes me so happy and gives me energy. I am already making a mental list of 'time guzzlers' that I plan to cut back on after this weekend. This will help me build more quiet time into my schedule for reading.

NEW MORNING RITUALS

I return home with a notebook full of remarks and recommended reading tips that Wilbers added during our walk together. I set my alarm to go off an hour earlier the next morning. It is 6 a.m. and I realize that the prospects of tons of reading time and this new ritual are really good for me. No time to read? Nonsense! How many more books will I be able to finish if I adopt this new habit? At this time of day, it's really nice to be disconnected from the outside world; no one expects anything from me. I grab a blanket, make a cup of fresh ginger tea

and set the timer on my phone for an hour; this was also a tip from Wilbers that works well for me.

In order to hold onto the mood from the weekend, I start reading *The Heart is a Lonely Hunter*. Before I know it, the story of four people in search of something, who, in all their restlessness and loneliness, end up at the one bar that is open in the darkest of night, has taken hold of me. McCullers' style is unique; she observes, without embellishment, yet is not distant. I dog-ear numerous pages and on the second day, I once again read one of those 'Yes!' sentences, and it's not even one uttered by one of the main characters. In answer to her father's question about what her brother has done this time, Portia responds, 'Just wait a minute. Just let me find brain room so I can study it all out and tell it to you plain.' ●

WANT TO EXPERIENCE MORE?

* Listen: 'Lover, Beloved: Songs from an Evening with Carson McCullers', by Suzanne Vega (Amanuensis Productions)

* Check out: readingretreat.co.uk (UK only) for some great reading retreat inspiration. Or try bookriot.com/airbnb-reading-retreat for places in the US.

* Get inspired: '10 Gorgeous Retreats Perfect for a Quiet Reading Weekend' blog on novelicious.com, or 'Reading Retreats: Paradise for Book Lovers' on salon.com

* The School of Life also offer reading retreats and bibliotherapy sessions. Theschooloflife.com

Clementine Churchill

SHE PLAYED A LARGE AND INFLUENTIAL ROLE IN THE POLITICAL CAREER OF HER HUSBAND, WINSTON CHURCHILL. BUT THE FLAMBOYANT AND AMBITIOUS CLEMENTINE CHURCHILL-HOZIER WOULD MUCH RATHER HAVE BEEN A STATESWOMAN IN HER OWN RIGHT.

They first met at a ball in 1904. Clementine (rhyming with 'lean', not 'line') Hozier was a nineteen-year-old, bookish and aristocratic young woman; Winston Churchill was thirty, a young politician whose star was rising fast. She stood half a head taller than he, and wasn't any good at small talk. He, as always in the company of a pretty woman, was at a loss for something to say. There was no immediate spark.

Four years later, in March 1908, their paths crossed again at a dinner party, and there was an instant connection. Winston—now a member of the British Parliament—realized she was a beautiful woman who was easy to talk to, and she found him quite dashing. Things moved fast this time, and they were married in London on September 12 that year. According to Clementine's biographer, Sonia Purnell, the wedding ceremony was indicative of what her future would look like, because as they were signing the marriage register, Winston walked off to enter into an animated political discussion with his fellow politician David Lloyd George, who would become British Prime Minister eight years later.

Winston Churchill, the resolute British Prime Minister who brought the Germans to their knees in WWII, became the hero of his era. Far less is known about Clementine, but we have a lot to thank her for. Without Clementine at his side, Winston would never have made it that far in life. She believed in him, and he needed that. In addition, she compensated for his shortcomings, prevented him from making mistakes and gave him useful advice. So, who is this woman who had such an influence on world history?

EARLY OBSTACLES

Clementine Hozier was born in London on April 1, 1885. Her mother was Lady Blanche Hozier, a woman who did not take marital fidelity very seriously. Clementine's birth certificate states that her father is Colonel Henry Hozier, her mother's husband, but this wasn't true. The colonel didn't want children and Lady Blanche did, so she looked elsewhere to satisfy that need. Clementine, the second of four children, was a fearful and insecure girl. Lady Blanche was too wrapped up in her love life to spend a lot of time on her offspring and Clementine didn't get much attention from her 'father' either. He only showed an interest in the children at the time of the divorce, when he laid claim to them just to punish his soon-to-be ex. After a brief tug-of-war the children ended up with their mother, but because she wasn't receiving any alimony, they grew up in relative poverty. This left its mark on Clementine for the rest of her life.

Her childhood wasn't all misery and strife: Clementine was allowed to go to school—not yet very common for a girl in those days—and enjoyed it immensely. She even hoped for an academic career, but her mother put a stop to that. A 'bluestocking' (an intellectual woman) was unlikely to find a rich husband, and that's what was expected of her. When Clementine left school, she worked at her cousin's dressmaking business to earn a living—which was quite difficult for an aristocratic young woman. She was engaged a few times, but they never ended in marriage because she wasn't really in love. >

Clementine Hozier before she married Winston Churchill, 1908.

'If only I had been born with trousers rather than petticoats'

'When things really got unbearable,
Clementine would just take off for a few months'

A BEDROOM OF THEIR OWN

And then Winston Churchill appeared on the scene. With him, Clementine married for love. He was brilliant and funny, but also demanding, self-centered and rash. She was intelligent and perfectionistic, but could also be rigid and explosive. Things could get pretty heated in the Churchill home. The couple argued but they always stuck to the agreement they made on their honeymoon: All quarrels were reconciled before they went to sleep, each in their own bedroom. And when things really got unbearable, Clementine would just take off for a few months. Although Winston was consumed by his work, he always missed her dearly during her absences, according to their volumes of correspondence. In these letters, they referred to each other as 'Pug' (Winston) and 'Kat' (Clementine). They bonded with each other over politics as well as a difficult childhood with a promiscuous mother—something Winston had in common with his wife. He lived for the political arena and Clementine was equally ambitious. She once said she would have loved to have been a statesman in her own right if only she had been born with trousers rather than petticoats. Unfortunately, she lived in a time when women with such ambitions couldn't make it very far, so she made her husband's career into her life's work.

NO HOLDING BACK

Right from the start of their marriage, they were a strong team. Winston discussed everything with his 'Clemmie'

1. Clementine cutting the cake as the guest of honor at the annual Queen Charlotte's Ball in London, 1957.
2. Winston, Clementine and their daughter Sarah, 1933.
3. Clementine on one of her tennis vacations in Nice, France, 1923.
4. Clementine giving a speech during a football match to support the Red Cross and Russia, 1942.
5. Clementine with Marigold, a year before the little girl died.
6. Queen Juliana of the Netherlands receiving Clementine at a banquet in London, 1972. Queen Elizabeth II is standing on the right.
7. Winston and Clementine at the christening of their granddaughter Charlotte, daughter of Mary, 1954.
8. Winston greeting his wife after returning from a meeting with Stalin in Moscow. London, 1944.

and she had an opinion of her own to share with him. In many ways, she was more progressive. Clementine's psychological and political insights were very keen, often sharper than her husband's. He benefited from this—when he listened. Privately she didn't hold back, but in public she loyally seconded Winston's opinion. And so she developed not only into a perfect hostess, as was expected of a wife in those days, but also, more surprisingly, into his most trusted political adviser, his spin doctor and his most faithful lobbyist. Despite her shyness, Clementine would even staunchly campaign on Winston's behalf when he was embroiled in affairs of the state. Their great goal was to make him Prime Minister of Britain. And it wasn't an easy road. During WWI, Winston, as First Lord of the Admiralty, was jointly responsible for the dramatic failure of the Gallipoli campaign and he had no choice but to resign.

After that his political career went up and down, and in the 1930s he was even sidelined because of his aversion to Nazi Germany—which at that time wasn't shared by the majority in Britain. Clementine was totally dedicated to her domineering husband and not capable of paying much attention to anything or anyone else. As their daughter Mary would later say, "For her, father always came First, Second and Third". But living with Winston wasn't easy. Clementine was often depressed and gloomy and she would go away for months on end to recover her spirits, playing a lot of tennis, even when her children were still very young. She didn't know any better, having herself hardly known motherly love. The death of their daughter Marigold at only two-and-a-half years of age was, in a way, a turning point. Mary, the fifth and youngest child of the Churchills, was born a year later, in 1922, and was watched more closely.

MOST COURAGEOUS DEED

The outbreak of WWII finally showed Winston had been right about Hitler. It was clear who should lead Britain in the coming battle, and Winston was finally made Prime Minister. During the war, the Churchills experienced their finest hour. He worked day and night, and so did Clementine, who under these difficult circumstances was a tireless example of tranquility and courage. She was her husband's direct line >

Sonia Purnell is Clementine Churchill's most recent biographer, and her book 'First Lady: The Life and Wars of Clementine Churchill' was a great source of information for this feature

'At the age of 80, Clementine finally was a "statesman". Sadly, it was too late'

to the people: She visited bomb shelters and she edited his now-famous speeches, making sure that they avoided long words that would be hard to understand. In order to win the war, the Americans had to be persuaded to participate, and this was a task that both Churchills tackled very earnestly. The top American diplomats whom they received at their home were impressed by Winston's charisma and Clementine's culinary prowess. When their daughter Sarah started an affair with the American ambassador, they didn't object—quite the opposite. The national interest went above everything. That's why Clementine also kept quiet when in 1943 she was told by Winston's personal physician that his state of health was so bad that he might succumb to a fatal heart attack at any moment. She wanted him to be able to continue his important work without any worries. According to Sonia Purnell, that was 'arguably her most decisive—and courageous—act of the war'.

LAST ROUND

Winston was hailed as a hero after the WWII victory. Yet his party was defeated in the general elections and, in 1945, Winston was no longer Prime Minister. It was difficult for the Churchills to digest this turn of events. What now, without an enemy to defeat, a government to lead or a people to fire up with courage? They spent a lot of time apart, although their love remained strong. On September 12, 1948, in honor of their 40th wedding anniversary, Winston wrote, 'My Beloved, I send this token, but how little can it express my gratitude to you for making my life and any work I have done possible'.

Unexpectedly, at the age of 76, Winston, despite his bad health (still anxiously kept secret), became Prime Minister again. Clementine remained the devoted wife, but she barely involved herself with politics anymore. Her health was poor, and she was somber and short-tempered. Instead, she spent more time with her children and grandchildren and enjoyed it immensely. She even told her daughter Mary during one of their picnics, "I see you having such fun with your children and I missed out on that with all of mine".

A QUIETER LIFE

In 1955, Winston's political career reached its end, and he resigned. The final farewell to the political arena was notably more difficult for Clementine than for Winston. He, as a former statesman, was still showered with the attention of admirers and also had other interests to pursue—his painting and the much-beloved country house of Chartwell (to which Clementine was indifferent). Her life became quieter; a woman who lives her life in service to her husband doesn't have many friends. The marital rhythm of the Churchills didn't change: They spent short periods together in London or Chartwell, and then traveled separately for long periods. The years were starting to show. In the 1960s, a black veil fell over the family: Winston's health deteriorated; their oldest daughter, Diana, committed suicide; and son Randolph, an unsympathetic man who according to contemporaries 'would pick an argument with a chair', drank himself to death. After the death of Winston in 1965, Clementine seemed to relax, according to the people around her. Apparently it was less taxing to care for his legacy, which of course she did actively, than for the man himself. Four months after his death, she was made baroness and in that capacity became a cross-bench member of the House of Lords. So at the age of 80, Clementine finally was a 'statesman'. Sadly, it was too late: She was too old to be able to put her stamp on anything. On December 12, 1977, at the age of 92, Clementine Churchill died of a heart attack at her London home. ●

WANT TO READ MORE?
....
* 'First Lady: The Life and Wars of
  Clementine Churchill', by Sonia Purnell
* 'Clementine Churchill: The biography
  of a marriage', by Mary Soames
  (her daughter)
* 'The Churchills: A Family at the Heart
  of History', by Mary S. Lovell

TEXT LIDDIE AUSTIN PHOTOGRAPHY ©MARY EVANS PICTURE LIBRARY 2015 (PHOTO 5 PAGE 54), GETTY IMAGES, HOLLANDSE HOOGTE BACKGROUND ILLUSTRATION SHUTTERSTOCK HAND-LETTERING VALESCA VAN WAVEREN

Clementine outside the Royal
Academy in London, 1931.

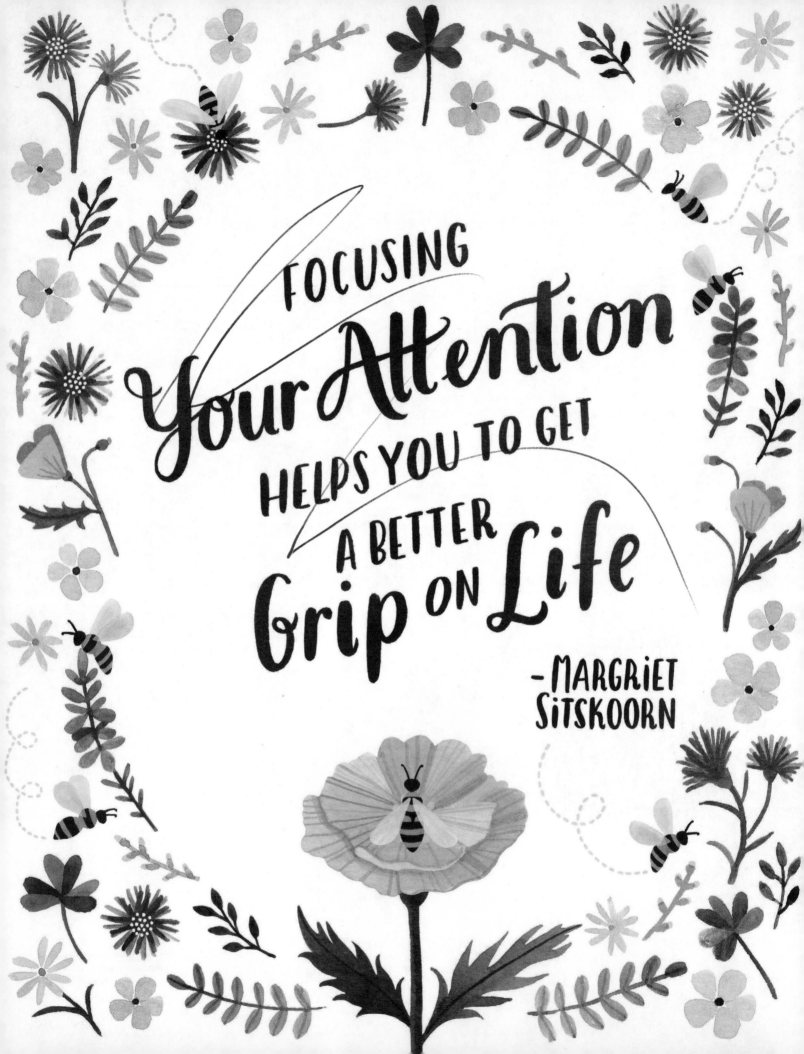

FOCUSING
Your Attention
HELPS YOU TO GET
A BETTER
Grip on Life

—MARGRIET
SITSKOORN

'Training your attention is empowering yourself'

We can teach ourselves to be less distracted
by the things that don't really matter.
Professor of Neuropsychology Margriet Sitskoorn
talks about how.

How would you describe the world we are living in?

It is a world that is complex, uncertain and changing rapidly. You used to go to the library to borrow a book, and in that book you could find the truth. You would then know exactly how everything worked, and things stayed the same for a very long time. That's all different now. Everything changes very quickly, and we also have this tsunami of information sweeping over us—not only from our immediate vicinity, but from all over the world and concerning rather major problems, like politics, the migration of displaced people, our climate. When something happens anywhere in the world, we know about it within seconds. So there's a lot going on, and that has an effect at all levels: emotionally, cognitively and physically. You can't possibly understand how everything works anymore.

So basically you're saying we can't keep up…

Yes, and it makes us insecure, because we have the idea that it's all very important, but at the same time we can't control it. This creates stress. What we really need to do is develop new and adequate ways to deal with this new world. For example, we used to tick things off our to-do lists and then start doing something else. But now the list is never finished. It continues to grow constantly and the flood of information—whether useful or distracting—also keeps coming. That beeping phone is not even the problem, it's the way we deal with it and let ourselves be continuously interrupted. So we need to learn new skills to regain control over our own lives.

How does the brain deal with all the stimuli and temptation?

The story of the brain begins in ancient times and it has evolved over eons. A lot of what was in the brain in the old days is still there, because the brain has evolved in layers. The pain and pleasure centers of our brain are stimulated when we are exposed to things that are necessary to survive and to reproduce the species, such as food, possessions and sex. So when you are confronted with fat, salt, sugar, information or someone with whom you could have sex, the pleasure center is stimulated deep in the brain. It happens as soon as the possibility of pleasure is present. This system worked very well in times of scarcity and when society was less complex.

How has this now become problematic?

We now live in times of plenty, and the possibility of pleasure is always present in our lives: We can eat, drink, have sex, buy things, work, be in touch with our friends and so on, 24 hours a day. Consider what that means for those ancient structures in the brain: they are being triggered all the time. They are short-term systems, because when something was scarce, we had to act immediately. So now we are getting the signal to act immediately all day long. 'Look, pizza: Eat it immediately.' 'New information: Absorb it immediately.' And this is why sometimes we drink alcohol, cheat on our partner, work >

'BEING ABLE TO DIRECT YOUR ATTENTION WHERE YOU WANT IT IS A TREMENDOUSLY IMPORTANT SKILL IN THIS AGE'

too much, are always eating sugary foods and are inclined to continually respond to all of the stimuli and information that crosses our path.

But surely we have some control over our behavior?
In the course of evolution, naturally, there have been quite a few changes. The newest development in our brain is the prefrontal cerebral cortex, which enables us to more or less regulate the other areas in the brain, especially the pleasure area. With this new region, you can do things like make plans, focus your attention, learn from feedback, make complex decisions, control emotions and suppress impulses. So that prefrontal cortex can say: 'Very tasty pizza, but I'm not going to eat it immediately'. Now you can stop yourself from buying everything, working too much or looking at your phone all the time.

And how does that work in practice?
The brain actually works in a very simple way: it is exposed to a stimulus to which you react. But what do we need in these modern times? Not the automatic and immediate response, but a kind of moment or space that lets you think a bit, which encourages the right reaction. Maybe it won't be completing your to-do list, but just sitting back and catching your breath. Or going for a walk in the woods. The prefrontal cerebral cortex doesn't simply make you say 'No!' all day long either. It's responsible for letting you

decide sometimes that you don't need to do something immediately—because you may have a different goal—and at other times, 'Okay, let's do it'. So a balance is established between the short-term enjoyment and the long-term happiness, and you can set your priorities.

So it's good to understand how it works in the brain?
I think it's extremely important, because most of us don't even realize that we are constantly responding to stimuli. We think we're making our own decisions, like deciding to look at our phone two hundred times a day. But the moment the device beeps, lights up or vibrates, your attention is already on it before you have made the decision to focus your attention on it—simply because the brain has been developed to work in that way. We also know from research that a lot of people are already so triggered by that phone that they even look when it's not doing anything. Only when you realize that and admit it to yourself, can you do something about it. Because you can turn off your phone, or turn the sound off. That already fades out some triggers.

You have written that attention is one of the most important skills we need in this time...
It is often said that what you give attention to grows in importance. And that is so true. Attention is very important for what you perceive and therefore what you feel, think and develop. That's because it directs the

plasticity of your brain: attention gives, as it were, a signal to your brain that says, 'This is important, I need to do something with this'. As a result, the brain commits itself to doing something with what you have focused on. Being able to direct your attention where you want it is a tremendously important skill in this age, where you encounter hundreds of thousands of things every day that you could theoretically respond to. If you can consciously focus your attention on something and then hold, divide or let go of that attention at will, you will be distracted by the stimuli from your environment or from yourself less often. You will also have less trouble completing tasks, and won't spend much time on things or thoughts that aren't useful anymore.

You have become a great supporter of attention training.
I must admit, I was a non-believer at first. But scientific research has shown how beneficial attention training, such as meditation or mindfulness, is for the brain. It's logical: If you can't regulate your own attention you can't regulate your life. You go into town without needing anything, and suddenly you're hungry for chicken because of that nice smell wafting out of the restaurant kitchen, and you want new shoes because you see them in the shop window. You end up wanting all kinds of things. By training your attention, you are empowering yourself to not react to everything—not to each and every shiny thing in the outside world, and

WE ALL NEED Space TO Think a Bit

INTERVIEW **SJOUKJE VAN DE KOLK** ILLUSTRATIONS **VALESCA VAN WAVEREN**

sometimes also not to your own thoughts and emotions. So that you can determine for yourself what is important and what isn't.

And everyone can become better at this?
My specialty is neuroplasticity, the adaptability of the brain. Everyone can indeed become better at this, because the beauty of the brain is that it can develop and change. The more you develop these executive skills, as they're called, the easier it becomes to be successful in the broader sense of the word. You'll be healthier and happier, contribute more to the lives of others, be more content with your salary and you will become better at maintaining your family and other relationships. Because if you just keep on going in a life that you don't have personal control over, it will have major consequences: burnout, divorce or alcoholism, for example. Plus, chronic stress—constantly feeling that you must handle things but can't and can't actually escape them either—literally breaks the brain. So it is vital to take charge of your life again.

Your vision is that we can and must take matters into our own hands. But what if that doesn't work?
That is indeed my message—especially because we have become like leaves turning in the wind without being aware of it. There are attention-grabbers everywhere and always, so you have to learn how to manage what you focus on, otherwise you probably won't be doing the things you really want to. That is why it's my mission to make people more aware of what's happening, what the impact on the brain is and what influence you can have yourself. Maybe you won't reach your goal, but at least you won't fail because you have fallen into the trap of being distracted by things that you didn't even want to do. And if you can't find a way to manage, find some help. There are all kinds of training courses, apps and programs that can help in a way that suits you.

What is your most important advice for preventing stress?
Keep track of the things that are running your life, because that insight can help you to do something about it.

And be honest about it. For example, keep track of how often you really look at your phone. And what does it do to you when you put your phone away for a day? Or try to find out whether you are being guided by the things that really matter to you or by your to-do list. Also, write down what is most important in your life and then what you spend your time on. A lot of people turn out to be spending most of their time on their work, while the things that matter most are last on the list: children, health and friends. This simple exercise gives insight into how you really lead your life. And once you have that, you can go on to do things differently from now on. ●

....

MARGRIET SITSKOORN (1966) is a neuropsychologist and professor of clinical neuropsychology. She is also the author of several books on how the brain works, such as 'Train Your CEO Brain: And Become Your Best Self'.

....

Pastry chef Roberto and his sister Samia in El Riojano

FAMILY TIES IN MADRID

What stories from around the world are we not hearing about on TV or in the news? In this series, correspondents write about their experiences in the countries where they live. Here, Madrid-based Hagar Jobse discusses the Spanish belief in putting family first.

If I tell my Dutch friends that I call my family once a day, I usually get strange looks. Most of them only speak to their families once a week or so, or every other week. I have been living in Madrid for four years now, and for my Spanish friends, it's completely normal for me to call my parents every day and that my sister and I regularly have Skype open as 'background noise' as we both stand in our respective kitchens and cook. Back home in the Netherlands however, the closeness of the family I grew up in is more the exception than the rule.

In Spain, it's the most normal thing in the world to put your family's interests first. A friend of mine who lives in Madrid but is originally from Tenerife flew to the island of her birth every weekend for a year to be with her mother who was seriously ill. It cost a fortune, but it was worth it. Even though her mother is doing better now, they still speak on the phone three times a day, and she gets on a plane to go visit her once a month. The economic crisis taught me another meaning of the concept of family. In 2013, during the low point of the crisis, over 27 percent of Spaniards were out of a job. Half of all young people were unemployed. Who helped these people? That's right: their families. Sometimes children, grandchildren and grandparents would all live in one house in order to make ends meet.

When it comes to work, family also appears to act as a huge safety net in Spain. Don't be surprised if you meet a bartender who studied law or an art historian working behind the counter at a butcher's shop. When the crisis had just begun, many children went to work in their parents' business. This was a win-win for both generations. After all, the children aren't sitting at home unemployed and the parents are relieved that they don't have to close the doors of the business, allowing the family tradition to continue.

FLAMENCO GUITARS

The walls of the Pedro de Miguel guitar store are filled with photos of all the flamenco greats who once tried out a guitar there. When you enter the store, you can >

'The majority of the Spanish companies that came through the economic crisis so well are family businesses'

see right into the workshop at the back where the guitars are made. Rubén Pérez is helping a customer while Álvaro Rodriguez replaces the strings on a guitar. This amazing store in the centrally located district of Huertas owes its survival to the younger generation. Rubén's father opened the workshop together with Miguel Ángel Rodriguez in 1991. They decided to specialize in flamenco guitars and are now well-known among flamenco musicians. "People come to us because they know they can get good handmade products here," says Rubén. Álvaro is also a student, so he only works in the store two hours in the afternoon. "Information science is another love of mine, but in today's job market, it's better to have as many options as you can," Álvaro explains. Even if he ends up working in the family business later, he doesn't see it as a drawback. "Guitars are beautiful instruments. I would love to be able to work with them every day. It is comforting to know that I can always work in the store if I can't find another job." Rubén, Álvaro and Miguel Ángel all believe there are other advantages to working with family. "We don't have to hide it for very long when we're irritated," Rubén says. "You're usually more honest and direct with family than strangers. It's good to be able to clear the air and focus on work again."

KEEPING THE STORE OPEN

Rubén has been in the store every day since he was fourteen, helping out after school. He never thought he would take over the business, but when his father died nine years ago and Miguel Ángel asked him to come work at the store, Rubén didn't have a moment of doubt. "I had been working as a chef for five years and was tired of being in the kitchen," he says. "I needed to do something else. We also work long days here but this work is a lot less stressful. Aside from that, my decision was partly based on my emotions. I knew that if I didn't work in the business, Miguel Ángel would eventually have to close it down. You need a lot of patience to work in this business, and it's not an easy trade to learn. Training someone would just take too long and cost money. Miguel Ángel is like a father to me so I really wanted to help him."

FAMILY OF COBBLERS

According to Daniel Lorenzo, an expert on family businesses and an academic researcher, this loyalty is actually one of the main reasons family businesses are doing so well. "The majority of the Spanish companies that came through the economic crisis so well and continue to grow now are family businesses," he explains. "People have a very strong sense of responsibility here and often do anything to avoid having to fire staff, even if it means making less profit."

Cristian Larrañaga can relate. He comes from a family of cobblers, and the home he grew up in was above his father's store. "My family is like a commune for me," he says. "My mother worked in the store and my uncles in the workshop. I was acutely aware of the fact that our product, shoes, is what put food on the table and I have always felt responsible for the business." Cristian studied political science but stopped after a couple years. "The people I knew who did finish the study program were either unemployed or went abroad to find work. I wondered what kind of future lay ahead for me. This was why I decided to stop and go work for my father." His younger brother, Denis, also works in the store.

When their father, Jorge, opened his store 36 years ago, he also did it in his family's best interests. "Back when I was young, the cobbler profession was really hard," Jorge says. "You couldn't get a contract anywhere. My father worked as a freelancer and could suddenly find himself without work. We didn't have a lot of money." Initially, Jorge didn't want to become a cobbler. He held a variety of administrative positions at different companies for years. When he was 30, he decided that he wanted his father to have more economic stability in his later years, and suggested opening a shoe repair store together. The business took off immediately. Jorge also decided to design his own line of shoes. "I am a real self-taught man," he laughs. "Sure, I already knew something about making shoes, but I had never designed shoes before."

Jorge learned the business through trial and error, worked on commission for an array of famous Spanish designers and even designed the shoes for international >

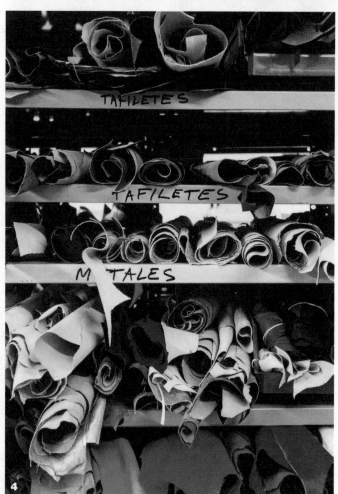

1. Álvaro, Miguel Ángel and Rubén in the workshop of the Pedro de Miguel guitar store.
2. Pastry chef Roberto in front of El Riojano, founded in 1855 by the pastry chef of Queen Isabella II of Spain.
3. Cristian and Denis with their father Jorge in the studio.
4. The Larrañagas still cut the leather with a knife and not a laser.

'A family business gives you security that many other people don't have'

Rubén behind the counter of guitar store, Pedro de Miguel

movies such as *The Danish Girl* and popular Spanish TV series. He is one of the few people left in Madrid who still makes shoes by hand. In spite of this, his sales have been down by 30 percent since 2008 when the economic crisis began. His sons are now helping him to focus on the international market. "They have set up a web shop and are looking for partnerships with magazines. That's their thing; I'm more old-school, word-of-mouth and so on. Thanks to this web shop, we have already had orders from a customer in Switzerland and a few from the UK."

COMPLETE TRUST

"I have seen so many companies like this go out of business," says Esperanza Comontes, owner of pastry shop El Riojano. "If the children don't want to take over the business, that's it, end of story." El Riojano has beautiful marble floors and a classic interior. Typical sweet Spanish treats are neatly laid out in a wooden display case with decorative gold accents. It's impossible to find a more attractive pastry shop in Madrid. A bronze plaque with 'Est. 1855' hangs over the door. The story behind the opening of this pastry shop is also amazing, as it was the personal pastry chef of Queen Isabella II of Spain who opened it. The queen herself provided the funds to open the shop; she wanted to support her favorite chef in the next step in his career.

El Riojano is a household name in Madrid. From the minute the doors open, the shop is packed. Elegantly dressed older Spanish ladies love to come here for a cup of coffee and a pastry. "I used to come here with my mother when I was a little girl," an older lady says in passing. Esperanza doesn't have to worry about the future of El Riojano. Her children Samia, Roberto and Marta all work there and she's confident one of them will be prepared to continue the tradition. Samia helps out by waiting tables and working the register, Roberto is the pastry chef and Marta is responsible for the bookkeeping and hiring extra staff. "There is no employee I trust as much as my own children," Esperanza says. "Besides, you have to be willing to make a lot of sacrifices if you are going to work for us. We are open seven days a week and it is a madhouse here,

ABOUT THE CORRESPONDENT

Hagar Jobse lives in Madrid and works for the Dutch online platform *De Correspondent* as well as *Al Jazeera English*. "From the time I was fifteen, I knew that I would end up living in Spain," he says. "My mother studied Spanish language and culture and we always went to Spain on vacation. I love the people and the spontaneity of the country. You can always make plans with friends at the last minute. I love that. I studied Spanish, history and journalism. In between, I lived in Granada for a few months and in Madrid for a year. A little over three years ago, I decided to try to work as a freelance journalist in Madrid. It turned out to be a good decision. I don't have any plans to go anywhere for the time being."

particularly during the holiday season. There aren't many people willing to do this." She believes that her children are privileged to be able to work at the pastry shop. "In the current job market, if there's a family business you can work for, you should consider yourself lucky. It gives you security that many other people don't have."

The two oldest children have always wanted to work at El Riojano and started their jobs there right after graduating from high school. Even the youngest daughter, Marta, who studied art history, is happy that she has the chance to focus on the bookkeeping and personnel policy. "My dream is to be a museum curator," Marta says. "The only problem is that I couldn't take the mandatory national exam for seven years because there were no jobs during the crisis. During that time, I started working for my mother, and this was a good thing since the question was whether or not I would have gotten a job somewhere else." ●

TEXT **HAGAR JOBSE** PHOTOGRAPHY **NUNO PERESTRELO**

Who is Rupi Kaur?

**POET RUPI KAUR MADE HER BREAKTHROUGH
ON INSTAGRAM. WHEN SHE COMPILED HER POEMS AND
ILLUSTRATIONS INTO A BOOK, IT BECAME A BESTSELLER
WORLDWIDE. WE WANTED TO GET TO KNOW HER BETTER.**

What really makes Rupi Kaur so unique is that she made it to number one on *The New York Times* bestseller list with her poetry debut *milk and honey* entirely on her own. She found her own audience without pursuing the usual channels of literary magazines, the publishing world and literary reviews.

The idea to compile her poems and publish them as a book had actually never occurred to her. For Kaur, poetry was something she created for others to hear, first as a musical band and later touring as a performer. This approach may be traced back to her roots in India: When she was four, she and her family moved from Punjab to Canada, ultimately settling in Toronto. Born into a Sikh family, this was the tradition Kaur grew up with. As a child, she was accustomed to reciting ritual texts, lines of poetry set to music, with other people.

When Kaur started writing her own texts, very personal poems addressing themes such as family, love and heartbreak, giving performances reciting this poetry was the most natural thing for her to do. She went on tour, visiting college campuses where she found an audience of kindred spirits. Occasionally, she posted sound or video recordings on YouTube or SoundCloud. She didn't see paper as a suitable medium for communicating her message. This gradually changed when she started posting her poems on social media. >

COMMOTION ON INSTAGRAM

In 2015, Rupi Kaur posted a photo on Instagram, the intention of which, much like her poems, was to expose the attitude toward women and girls in Western society. The photo depicted stains on her sweatpants and her bedsheets from her period. Instagram felt the image was inappropriate and deleted it. Kaur argued that Instagram has no problem with allowing massive amounts of photos of women's 'pornified' bodies, but apparently refuses to approve images that portray women's natural physicality. She was widely applauded for her response, and was later allowed to repost the photo. Thanks to this incident, many new people discovered Kaur's poetry and became fans. She was able to continue to share her story the way she prefers to.

'Kaur strikes a chord with an entire generation'

HONEST AND REALISTIC

Tumblr was the platform where she first started sharing her poetry with friends and family. She quickly also got lots of followers outside of her own 'inner circle'. In 2013, she made the switch to Instagram where her follower numbers rose even faster, currently totaling around three million. She realized that as an Insta-poet, her poems had to be more direct than they were during her spoken-word performances. This led to the powerful style she is now famous for. She also added her own illustrations.

In response to the many requests she received, Kaur put together a book of her poems and illustrations, and self-published it. To her great surprise, the collection was a hit. She decided to work with a publisher, and the book shot to the top of the American sales charts. What appeals to so many readers about Kaur's work is that she writes about familiar and intimate themes such as love, family, heartbreak, abuse, survival, strength and sex, and does so using metaphors and observations.

She is honest and realistic, choosing a form of short dialogs that seem to be taken from her own life. Some critics feel that her poetry isn't very deep or literary, but the fact that Kaur strikes a chord with an entire generation indicates that there truly is more to it than appears. Now and then her poems contain some rather obvious lines, such as when she writes: 'If you are not

enough for yourself / you will never be enough / for someone else', but often Kaur manages to express a simple thought in a very poignant and original fashion. This is also evident in her poems on colored women: 'Our backs / tell stories / no books have / the spine to / carry'. A fashion designer embroidered this text on the back of a jacket; an ultimate expression of how poetry, social media and popular culture can become interwoven with one another. It also shows how poetry is returning more and more to the street where it is accessible for everyone, a concept that is fully in line with Kaur's ideas. She had the following to say in an article published in *Entertainment Weekly*: 'Poetry is amazing, and it should be mainstream, and I hope that it can only move in that direction more and more.' ●

WANT TO SEE MORE?

_____

* Read:'milk and honey'
  and 'the sun and her
  flowers', by Rupi Kaur
* Visit: Rupikaur.com
* Follow: @rupikaur_

_____

the sun
and her flowers

rupi kaur

TEXT **CHRIS MUYRES** PHOTOGRAPHY **©RUPI KAUR** HAND-LETTERING **VALESCA VAN WAVEREN**

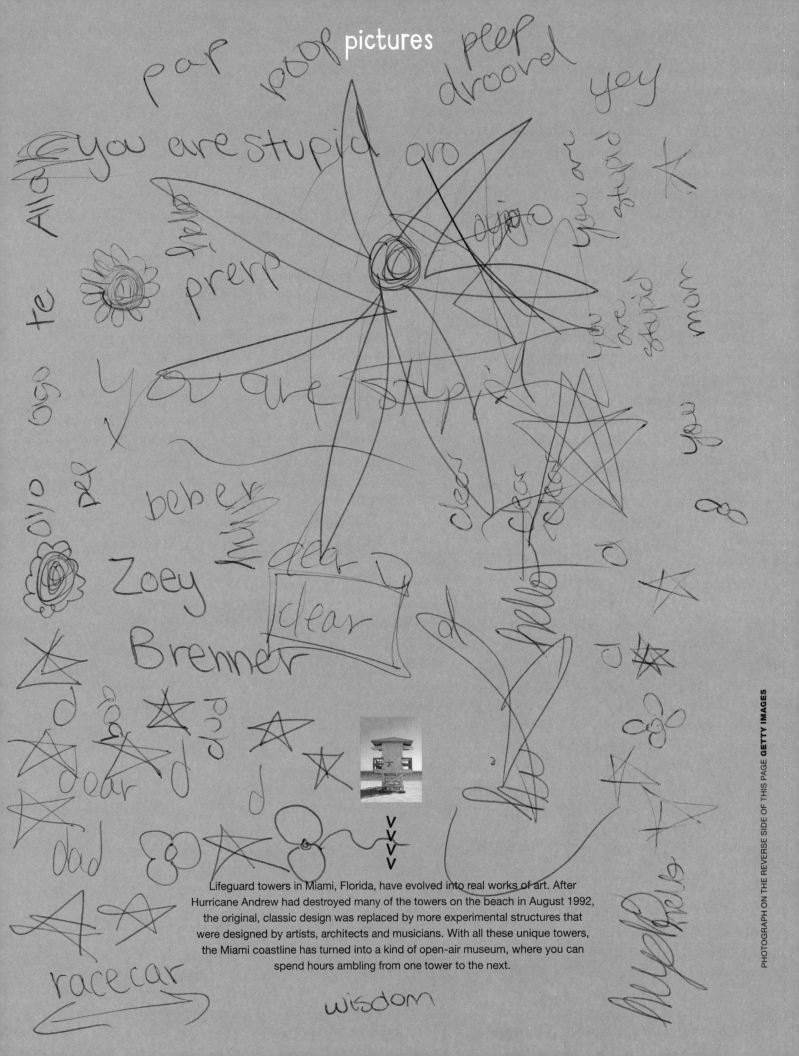

Lifeguard towers in Miami, Florida, have evolved into real works of art. After Hurricane Andrew had destroyed many of the towers on the beach in August 1992, the original, classic design was replaced by more experimental structures that were designed by artists, architects and musicians. With all these unique towers, the Miami coastline has turned into a kind of open-air museum, where you can spend hours ambling from one tower to the next.

My Sky, Your Sky

The assignment: Draw the sky on August 13, 2017, at 12 p.m. Eastern Standard Time. Illustrators all over the world looked up at that same moment. Their participation yielded a special collection of illustrations, some of which we share with you here.

Elsa Jenna (Montreal, Canada)

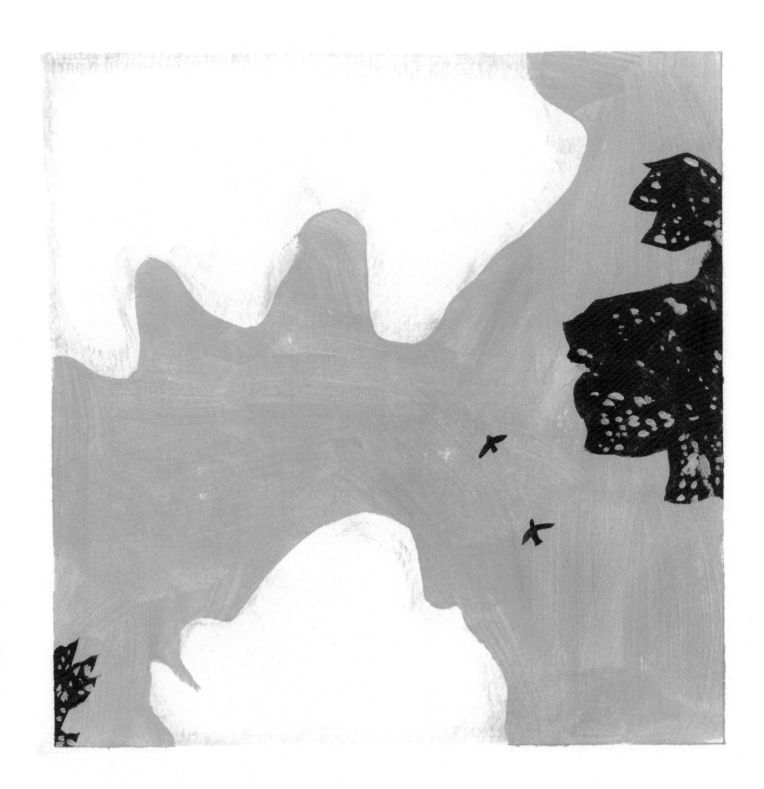

Penelope Dullaghan (Indianapolis, US)

>> Right-hand page, from left to right and from top to bottom:
Paula Rusu (Buftea, Romania), Jenny Volvovski (Chicago, US),
Chelsea O'Byrne (Vancouver, Canada), Kaylani Juanita McCard (Fairfield,
US), Renata Galindo (Mexico City, Mexico), Jianan Liu (Beijing, China)

Andrea D'Aquino (New York, US)

Marcelilla Pilla (Ohakune, New Zealand)

Leah Goren (Rockaway Beach, New York, US)

'I wanted to represent the cloudy sky
as realistically as possible. It was too good
to turn it into something about myself'

Elsa Jenna

The sky: We walk under it every day yet rarely look at it. But when you think back to your childhood or past vacations, the skies of that time often trigger memories. You can hear this, for example, in a radio interview with the American singer Rickie Lee Jones, when she was asked, "What did clouds look like when you were young?" Immediately she started to muse about the 'skies that went on forever' and 'little fluffy clouds', about how sunsets set the sky on fire, and how the clouds then caught the colors.

That skies strike a chord with many people is also evident in the One Sky project by Women Who Draw (womenwhodraw.com). Each month, the creative platform asks a number of connected illustrators to do something under the hashtag #WWDTogether. This time the idea was to look up at the sky at a fixed time and draw it, wherever in the world the illustrators were. The result: 88 illustrations that all show a highly personal piece of one and the same world sky.

One of the participants was Canadian Elsa Jenna, who has a Lee Jones-like bond with the skies of her youth. "As a child, every night I saw a row of three beautiful stars from my bedroom window—Orion's Belt—and I remember thinking then: these stars are mine," she says. "Whenever I see it today, it always brings me back to that peaceful time in my life. It reassures me."

Milja Praagman, in the Netherlands, also took part: "In my picture book, *Moet je zien!* (Look at this!), the skies play a starring role," she says. "I really love the sky, the views and faraway vistas. I'm actually quite a dreamer, which is why I changed my workspace not so long ago. Before, I had a street-view and spent half the day staring through the window at what was happening out there. Now I work in the attic and can only see the sky. That's where I made my drawing, at six o'clock in the evening. I found the idea that illustrators from all around the world were looking up together at that same moment in time so wonderful."

For Marcelilla Pilla in New Zealand, the project resounded with 'We all live under the same sky', a saying in her native country of Colombia: "It means that we are all connected to each other anyway. Now I live in a small, remote place in New Zealand and have little contact with other creatives. One Sky felt like a date to drink coffee and paint with friends. For me, that moment was four o'clock in the morning in the middle of the freezing winter. I was outside in my pajamas. I wanted to convey that in my illustration. It's also as if I'm pointing up: Look, the moon looks like an empanada! Like you do with friends when you peer up at the sky together and have silly conversations about nothing in particular."

The sense of connection that One Sky gave the illustrators seems to be a common thread. "The project opened my eyes," says Jianan Liu from China. "At the moment I'm far from home and often look at the sky because I feel it connects me to my family. I always imagine that we're looking up at the same time."

Isn't it extraordinary how a simple illustration project can yield so much more than just a drawing? ●

TEXT **CHRIS MUYRES** HAND-LETTERING **VALESCA VAN WAVEREN**

WANT MORE CLOUDS?

* Check out cloudappreciationsociety.org if
  you love looking at clouds and the sky.
* 'The Invention of Clouds: How an Amateur
  Meteorologist Forged the Language of the
  Skies', by Richard Hamblyn
* 'The Cloud Collector's Handbook', by
  Gavin Pretor-Pinney

That Wood Be Nice

GLOBAL GOODIES THAT ARE JUST
A MOUSE CLICK AWAY.

1. Hand-painted wooden goldfinch brooch, €10–kirstinstride.etsy.com **2.** Wooden bracelet, €20–crowdyhouse.com **3.** Solid pinewood plant stand, €50–craftedbyoitenta.etsy.com **4.** Woodchuck journal, US$30–amazon.com **5.** Wooden digital camera, US$130–fathersfactory.com **6.** Birch bark confetti, CAN$6–makerhouse.com **7.** Echidna necklace, AUS$40–onehappyleaf.com

Spots and Stripes

ROARINGLY GOOD GIFTS

COMPILATION ANNE-MARIE REM PHOTOGRAPHY ©B. HARVEY/STOCKSY UNITED, ISTOCK

1. Handmade fold-over clutch, €115–2chicdesigns.etsy.com **2.** White tiger enamel pin, €9–cocowestillustration.etsy.com **3.** Wild mug, £5–johnlewis.com
4. Pinwheel cake topper, €7–pickthecake.etsy.com **5.** Leopard face-to-face bracelet, €114–nachbijoux.com **6.** Cath Kidston notebook, £12–magpiepoundbury.
co.uk **7.** Tote bag, €18–kerrisganeson.etsy.com

Please note that prices and items on websites may vary

Mini Posters

WE PUT TOGETHER A LITTLE COLLECTION OF WOMEN'S PORTRAITS FROM FOUR FEMALE ILLUSTRATORS. THESE MINI POSTERS LOOK GREAT WHEN FRAMED, BUT THEY ALSO WORK PROPPED UP ON A DESK OR WEDGED IN A MIRROR FRAME. YOU CAN EVEN SEND THEM AS A POSTCARD.

VIRGINIE COGNET

On her website, French illustrator Virginie writes about herself, '*J'illustre, je peins, j'écris, je fais de la mise en page et j'édite*' ('I illustrate, I paint, I write, I do layouts and I edit'). Her portraits of women often feature dogs and cats. And in Virginie's children's book illustrations, tigers drive cars, and cats and rabbits sunbathe on the beach.
Virginiecognet.ultra-book.com

JANET HILL

Janet's work often evokes a sense of nostalgia. Her paintings are also a bit mysterious and dreamy at times. This is probably because she loves watching old movies and looking at old photos. Janet lives in a Victorian-style house in Ontario, Canada, together with her dog Finnegan and her husband, with whom she also runs her studio. Their whole house is full of books.
Janethillstudio.com

BODIL JANE

Bodil Jane lives and works in Amsterdam, the Netherlands, where she loves looking around for beautiful things to inspire her. That can include anything: a nice rain jacket, a tiled veranda or a beautiful interior. The women that she draws often wear very detailed clothing, because Bodil is secretly in love with fashion.
Bodiljane.com

ANNE BENTLEY

Anne lives in the San Francisco area, on the west coast of the US. She was originally a painter, but a couple of years ago she started trying out some things on the iPad and has drawn almost everything in this manner ever since. This way she gets the ideas out of her head faster, and that works well for her.
Bentleyworks.us

THE FABRIC
of Life

An apartment in a converted shoe
factory in East London, UK, is the
perfect fit for antique textiles expert
Su Mason.

Su Mason's cupboards are piled high with ginghams, ticking, paisleys, linens and
French trims from Azerailles, with their original tags from the 1940s

Mason has had the desk since her daughters were small. The entomology is antique, bought by daughter Romilly at fairs.

Original Crittall windows and bare brick walls are reminders of the building's factory past. The cushion is made from a fragile 1920s French toile.

Romilly buys antique and dilapidated collections in French markets.

'It's far more interesting to be surrounded by things that have been made with care and have stories to tell'

Mason with Pepper the pug.

'Workwear is just as evocative as a
silk nightdress. They all played a role
in people's lives'

> 'Today's throwaway culture, where everything from clothes to furniture is seen as short-term and disposable, is anathema to me'

Since December 2013, Su Mason has been living in a converted shoe factory in East London, in the UK, close to what was once the heart of the East End rag trade. She shares her apartment with her pug, Pepper, and for part of the week with her eldest daughter, Romilly. The building's industrial past shows in the exposed pipes and ducts, bare brick walls and high Crittall windows designed to let in lots of light for its one-time factory workers, who used to make Clarks Shoes here.

In contrast to some slicker conversions nearby, Mason's home isn't a shrine to designer furniture and fast fashion. With two bedrooms, a small bathroom and a walk-in kitchen, the main living space doubles as a storeroom for rails of clothes and stacks of fabrics that Mason sells at markets and antique fairs.

Her stock includes monogrammed French linen sheets, women's workwear from WWII as well as more quirky finds, such as a peach silk nightdress from the 1920s, a glittering Biba sheath and a dusty hemmed Miss Haversham-like embroidered gown.

What do all these items mean to you?
I don't think we've ever lived in such a throwaway culture, where everything from clothes to furniture is seen as short-term and disposable. But living like that is anathema to me. It's far more interesting to be surrounded by things that have been made with care and have stories to tell. I'm surrounded by things that are part of life. Many of these clothes were made for special occasions and then packed away in a trunk in an attic. They make you think about the story behind it—not only who wore it, but also the seamstress who measured it up, selected a particular silk thread and then stitched it by hand. One of the things I specialize in is utility wear: women's dungarees and thick overalls that, conversely, would have been worn day in, day out, but women liked to patch with brighter scraps or embroider, to make them a little bit prettier and more individual.

Your interior fits in seamlessly with the unvarnished appearance of the factory. How did you achieve that?
We decorated the apartment primarily with secondhand market finds and hand-me-down furniture. The big farmhouse table was passed on by a friend, and we bought other items at markets in the UK and France. I travel a lot to buy fabrics. The framed butterflies and few pieces of taxidermy are antique. Romilly buys dilapidated collections and restores them and the boxes. And I made the cushion covers myself, out of squares of vintage linen, toile de Jouy fabric and pieces of dyed cloth that were too small to sell, or too special to part with.

You have a stall at London's Portobello Road market and can also be found at other antique and vintage fairs. Who are your customers?
Fashion students and designers, among others. I've sourced workwear that has been a big inspiration for Margaret Howell's designers. And I've just got in some beautiful 1950s ballet pumps with a unique shape that I think a shoe designer friend will love. Seamstresses for the theater and TV also come to me for clothes, plus era-accurate original buttons and thread, so that costumes look as authentic as possible.

Do you store all that stuff at home?
Yes, one room in the apartment is full of notions drawers, with cards of pearl buttons, military epaulettes and spools of thread that look almost new. I bought many of them at French markets. There's something so lovely about their intactness, some with the price—a few sous—pencilled on the back. ●
@sumasonlondon

TEXT **JO LEEVERS** PHOTOGRAPHY **PENNY WINCER**

life

>>>>>

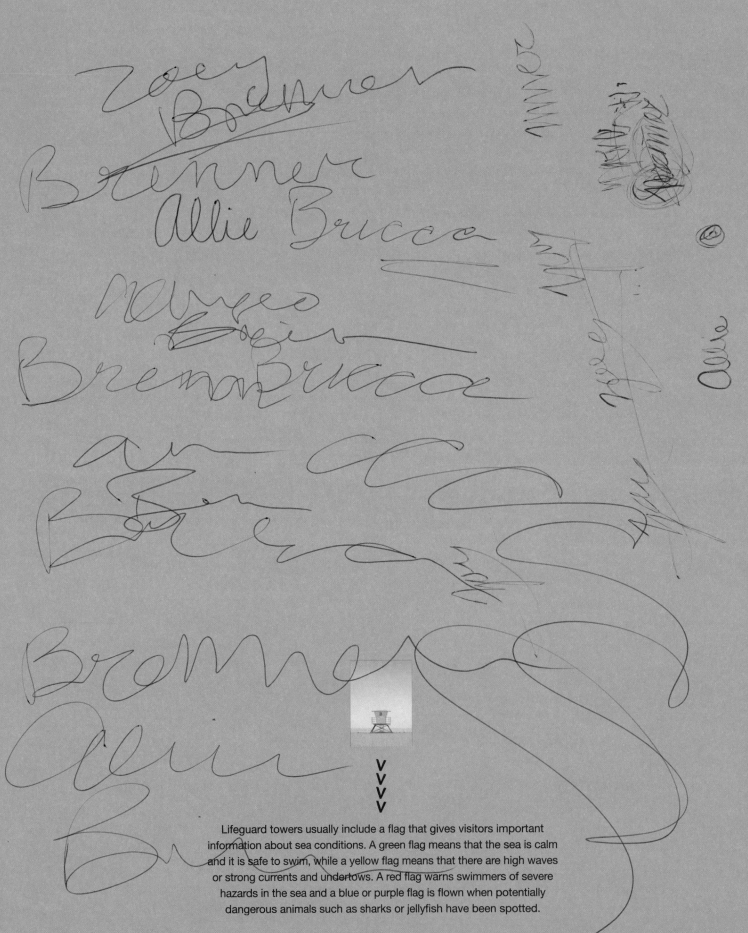

Lifeguard towers usually include a flag that gives visitors important information about sea conditions. A green flag means that the sea is calm and it is safe to swim, while a yellow flag means that there are high waves or strong currents and undertows. A red flag warns swimmers of severe hazards in the sea and a blue or purple flag is flown when potentially dangerous animals such as sharks or jellyfish have been spotted.

The Good Stuff
Favorite addresses, apps, books and more

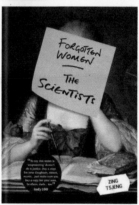

NO NONSENSE
As an inventor, maker and robotics enthusiast, you won't be surprised to learn that Simone Giertz is an avid fan of gadgets, but you may be surprised to hear that she's also an avid believer in making 'useless' things and how the outcome is far from useless as it helps us embrace and overcome failures and performance anxiety. You can watch her witty, heartfelt talk about the matter, 'Why You Should Make Useless Things', on ted.com.

PUTTING WOMEN (BACK) ON THE MAP
Through her illustrated *Forgotten Women* book series, Zing Tsjeng reveals and celebrates the amazing 'herstories' of influential women throughout history who have been overlooked or forgotten. From leaders and scientists to artists and writers, these women refused to accept the hand they were dealt and, as a result, shaped and changed the course of our futures, without any acknowledgement. Until now that is... Octopusbooks.co.uk

Productive Melodies

Looking for tunes to play while working—something calm that takes you away from the hustle and bustle without being a distraction itself? Here are some of our top tips:

* Ludovico Einaudi (e.g. *Islands— Essential Einaudi* album)
* Philip Glass (e.g. *Piano Works* and *The Hours*)

* Yann Tiersen (e.g. *Amélie* soundtrack)
* *Ella Fitzgerald Sings the Cole Porter Songbook*
* 'Requiem' by Gabriel Fauré
* Joep Beving (piano music)
* Wim Mertens (piano music)
* Erik Satie
* Vitamin String Quartet

Take Note

Whether you're a Bullet Journal user or not, you'll want to get your hands on *Metamorphosis* by Bridget Beth Collins (aka Instagram queen, Flora Forager) and transform it into a notebook that you can't be without. The dotted grid pages within are interspersed with the artist's signature compositions created using floral materials. With butterflies, moths, caterpillars, chrysalises and cocoons flitting through the journal, what better way to chronicle your every day and own life's transformation? Sasquatchbooks.com; Instagram: @flora.forager

As illustrator Lisa Congdon says: "You can always reinvent yourself". Which is exactly what she did when, aged 40, she left her teaching career to become a (now highly successful) artist. And in doing so, has inspired many others to do more with their creative side, not matter how old they are. Congdon has talked about this in various podcasts, and can now be seen on YouTube in Adobe Creative Cloud's show *Make It*, which talks to creatives to find out how they tick and what inspires their process.

AND FORWARD!

OFF THE BEATEN TRACK

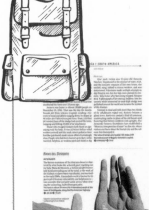

Atlas Obscura: An Explorer's Guide to the World's Hidden Wonders by Joshua Foer, Dylan Thuras and Ella Morton whisks you away on a mind-boggling journey to over 700 of the strangest, most curious places in the world. Celebrating the weird, the unexpected, the overlooked, the hidden and the mysterious, the book's pages are filled with fascinating portrayals, imagery and more, making it just as appealing to the armchair tourist as to the die-hard traveler looking for their next adventure. Workman.com

'A cup of tea would restore my normality'

From *The Hitchhiker's Guide to the Galaxy*,
by Douglas Adams (1952-2001), British author and dramatist

MINDFUL MOVEMENT

Relying on slow, continuous motion, Sway is an interactive meditation app that lets you find your own, most effective way to practice mindfulness in any given situation. Whether you're lying in bed, sitting at work, waiting for the train or taking a walk, simply moving your phone in your hand or gently swaying your body while using Sway helps you find focus in your everyday life.

TO REMOVE OR NOT TO REMOVE, THAT IS THE QUESTION...

Create poetic masterpieces with a little sneaky help from John Carroll's *Make Blackout Poetry*, a book filled with texts that you can repurpose for your own poems. Take the words of greats such as William Shakespeare, Jane Austen, Oscar Wilde and Victor Hugo, or even from vintage etiquette manuals, slang dictionaries, newspapers and more, and give them your twist by 'blacking' parts out to create your own ingenious remix.
Abramsandchronicle.co.uk;
Instagram: @makeblackoutpoetry

Tea Tales

Instead of throwing her used-up tea bags in the trash, artist Ruby Silvious uses hers as a canvas to create mini works of art that record her impression of a daily moment. The result is a collection of evocative, whimsical paintings, prints and collages—some of which have been compiled in her book, *363 Days of Tea: A Visual Journal on Used Tea Bags*—as well as tea-drinking-and-painting travels around the world. Rubysilvious.com; Instagram: @silvirub

A FLOWER A DAY...

For years, Sweden-based Juliane Solvång has been heading out for a walk every day from May to October, plucking a bunch of flowers along the way and posting a picture of it on Instagram. 'For me, the project is a kind of diary and part of my daily creative hygiene,' she writes. You can treat yourself to a bouquet-with-a-difference every day via her account, @onebouquetperday or even follow in Solvång's footsteps and post your own pickings with the hashtag #onebouquetperday.

finding some stillness in my mind

RANDOM THINGS SHE LIKES

Illustrator Nina Sprong-Minnaar tries to hold onto life's little pleasures for as long as possible. She used to keep a list of them, with little drawings, but felt like she wasn't doing the pleasures justice. "That's how I came up with the idea to post one 'bliss' on Instagram every Friday," she says. You can see her blissful drawings on @ninamaakt or #ninamaaktrandomthings.

'A room without books is like a body without a soul'

Cicero (106 BC-43 BC), Roman statesman and writer

BREAKING NEWS

Nowadays, we often find ourselves reading news that isn't always factually correct or complete because the media is in too much of a rush to be the first to break the story. As the world's first 'Slow Journalism' magazine, *Delayed Gratification* turns this frustrating issue on its head by revisiting the events of the previous three months to analyze the stories that mattered and see what has happened after the dust has settled. Get up to speed at slow-journalism.com.

Recipe for Disaster

Even though there's enough food on the planet to feed everyone, one third of the food produced each year is wasted and one in nine people go hungry every day. The World Food Programme (WFP) is addressing this issue with its #RecipeForDisaster social media campaign. Simply create a meal using ingredients near their sell-by date; take a photo; post the pic and recipe using the hashtag #RecipeForDisaster (tagging three friends to create their own) and make a donation to WFP to help combat food waste. Bon appétit. Wfp.org

From Boats to Bags

Mimycri is a Berlin-based brand that creates quality handmade products from plastic waste. But it's plastic waste with a history, as this social upcycling label works with refugees to make bags and backpacks from the broken, discarded rubber boats that have carried migrants to Greece. Sales of these products enable Mimycri to provide paid work to those who would otherwise have difficulty in finding some, and support other non-profit refugee organizations. Which means each bag is filled with a whole lot of good. Mimycri.de

TEXT **JULIA GORODECKY** IMAGES **LISA CONGDON** (SHARE THE FLAIR), **@SIMONEGIERTZ** (NO NONSENSE), **@GOODMIND&BODY** (RAW JOY), ISTOCK (PRODUCTIVE MELODIES), **LOUISE LOCKHART** (TO REMOVE OR NOT TO REMOVE, RECIPE FOR DISASTER), **SHUTTERSTOCK** (OFF THE BEATEN TRACK ILLUSTRATION, MINDFUL MOVEMENT, FROM BOATS TO BAGS), **DEBORAH VAN DER SCHAAF** (CAN'T JUDGE A BOOK BY ITS COVER)

CAN'T JUDGE A BOOK BY ITS COVER

Blind Date with a Book is a book that has been carefully curated from a wide range of popular genres, then hand wrapped and tagged with intriguing clues pertaining to the tome within. The collection ranges from books by great authors who you may have missed to ones that might not have received the publicity they deserved. You can pick your 'date' from blinddatewithabook.com or subscribe to their Book Club and enjoy a different rendezvous once a month for six months.

RAW JOY

According to a study at the University of Otago in New Zealand, if you're after that feel-good factor, you need to go raw. Researchers found that eating uncooked fruit and vegetables is more strongly associated with better mental health (mood, life satisfaction and drive) than consuming them cooked, canned or processed, as the latter can diminish nutrient levels, and therefore their benefits for optimal emotional functioning. The top ten raw foods related to this? Carrots, bananas, apples, dark leafy greens, grapefruits, lettuce, citrus fruits, berries, cucumbers and kiwis.

The Kindness of Strangers

She was never that keen on meeting new people, but when strangers appeared in her life, journalist Olivia Gagan started to change her mind.

There is a bookshop in Paris, France, called Shakespeare & Company. It is beautiful: old and narrow, with rickety wooden stairs and hidden corners that have played host to authors and poets, from Allen Ginsberg to Anaïs Nin. For decades, traveling writers have worked in the shop by day and slept among the shelves by night. The bookshop owners call these people 'Tumbleweeds'.

The shop's motto hangs on a sign above a door. It reads: 'Be not inhospitable to strangers, lest they be angels in disguise'. The message—to be welcoming and kind to those you don't know—is one I learned the meaning of last year, a year in which I accidentally became a sort-of tumbleweed, too, blown about on a journey around the world.

THE SAME, DAY IN, DAY OUT

I had spent the year before feeling, quite frankly, stuck. Stuck in a job in London, UK, that I had been in for years. Stuck in an apartment that was starting to feel too small for all the things I wanted to do with my life. I was tired of going to the same office day in, day out. Tired of taking the same route home. Tired of walking around the same places during my lunch break. All signs pointed to me needing to move on, to take some risks, but for some reason I couldn't work up the nerve to do it. I knew I was lucky to have no major problems—I had my health, wonderful friends, a roof over my head—but, still, I was dissatisfied. I was living life on a loop, and I was feeling cynical and bored.

I was also not particularly interested in welcoming newcomers into my world. I'm a sceptic by nature, questioning of everyone I meet. Instead of embracing strangers, I prefer to spend my time with friends I know well and love, relationships that have been decades in the making Strangers, whether they be romantic ones, potential new friends or maybe somebody new to work with, did not feature on my radar.

Which, in retrospect, might make it very clear why I found myself sitting at a bar with friends one night, pushing my drink around, complaining that nothing in my life was changing.

DANCING IN INDIA

And then—as tends to happen—fate started throwing out chances for me to grow; it was just up to me to notice, and take them. The first came when a colleague invited me to her wedding in Delhi. It was expensive, it would use up all my holiday time, I knew no one at the wedding other than the bride... but I went anyway.

India is not a country where you can easily be alone. In cities, there's no room for solitude: elbows jostle; hot, damp bodies press against each other; someone is shouting in your ear at every turn. Indian weddings, too, are big, beautiful, loud and lavish affairs. I arrived at the hotel where the three-day wedding was to take place and was immediately sent down to the gym. I wanted to rest up first in my room, but no: the bride informed me I needed to learn a dance routine, and fast.

This was because of the sangeet ceremony. It's a traditional part of an Indian wedding; a night where the guests perform music, dance and poetry for the bride and groom. So in a hot dance studio, I was learning >

> `'The smiling stranger had just spent 45 minutes helping me get back on my feet, and wanted nothing in return'`

a bhangra routine with the other guests, who ranged from students to school friends of the bride, and from Mumbaikars to New Yorkers.

Dance is an incredible way to get to know people. You are sharing physical space, working together to try and create something, to be in tune with each other. We were all in hysterics as we spun and shimmied, trying to memorize the routine for the following night. By the time the wedding ended, I'd danced, shared stories and talked for days—and realized how rarely I had bothered to make conversation with strangers in the past.

MISSING THE TRAIN
After the wedding, I decided to go to Darjeeling. Twenty-four hours on a sleeper train that would chug and puff its way through the foothills of the Himalayas, climbing thousands of feet to this temple of tea-making. I'd packed my diary, my camera and a book, and planned to spend the journey writing and taking photos of the Indian landscape as it passed by.

Except, trapped in Delhi traffic, I didn't make the train. I missed it by seconds—watched it pull out of the station—and stood on the platform, panicking. I couldn't read the signs posted around the vast, hot, dusty train station, and I was supposed to be meeting my host, 1,000 miles away and on the other side of the country, in exactly 24 hours.

Dripping with sweat, I hoisted my backpack which was about half my weight over my shoulder and

staggered into a waiting room to find a member of staff to help set me back on my way. After a few minutes of realizing there were about 50 other people waiting to ask for directions, I plonked myself down in a seat, in despair.

A man walked over to me, an American. "You look lost," he said, grinning. I must have looked ridiculous: a small, grumpy woman buckled down under the bulk of my backpack, face and arms covered with dirt and sweat. The last thing I needed was to make conversation with a fellow tourist, so I snapped back "I'm fine", hoping he would leave me to be confused and angry in peace. "Let me help you," he said. I was instantly suspicious, watching him warily as he sat down next to me.

This guy found a timetable. I had no Internet, no phone battery and there were no more trains that day for Darjeeling, and so he helped me find a cheap flight and a route to the airport. We walked over to the rickshaw stand, he made sure me and my gigantic backpack were safely stowed. He wished me well, and he was gone.

WALKING WITH A STRANGER
As the rickshaw rattled off toward the airport, I patted my bags to make sure he hadn't stolen something. He hadn't. The smiling stranger had just spent 45 minutes helping me get back on my feet, and wanted nothing in return. I felt embarrassed that I had automatically assumed he meant me harm.

India proved to be full of people willing to welcome me into their world. Once I finally made it to Darjeeling, a woman who worked at the hotel where I was staying offered to hike with me down through miles of tea plantations to a beautiful river.

As we walked, we talked, and it turned out she was the same age as me. I had grown up thousands of miles away in the UK, and she had never left Darjeeling. At first I wondered what on earth we'd find to talk about on the six-hour descent down the hills, but we ended up chatting all day. We talked about relationships and the difficulty of finding the right person. It turned out she loved movies and wanted my opinion on some we'd both seen. We both had ambitions with our work. As she talked, I realized I had once again made assumptions about a person I didn't know.

A CHAT EVERY DAY
I returned home from India feeling refreshed. Emboldened by all that travel, I decided to ask my boss if I could work for our company in Paris. To my complete surprise, he said yes. It meant three months living in a tiny apartment and working alone.

I constantly messaged my family and friends at home, and decided I wasn't going to be there long enough to meet anyone new. But once again, strangers decided to push their way into my life. There was a shop opposite my apartment stacked full of gorgeous things: soft woolen

pullovers, leather skirts, glittering dresses. I went in now and again, just to admire everything. The sales assistants got chatting to me one day, curious about my British accent. And so I started dropping in to chat, the women in patient French, me in bad French, stumbling over all my words.

By the end of my stay in Paris, I was sad to say goodbye to that shop. I hadn't bought a thing, but those women had given me the gifts of friendliness, conversation and seriously improved language skills.

They also made me question why I had become so closed off and hardened to new people in the past. I think it was a natural defense mechanism to a few relationships ending, a few rough experiences—and so I had scuttled away and retreated into my shell. Not believing in the kindness of strangers is no way to live long-term, though. At some point, you have to peep back out of your shell and try again.

My last lesson came on a vacation in Mexico. I was too scared to jump into a cenote, a deep natural pool carved out of a cave, filled with beautiful, icy water. I applauded as my friend jumped in from a ledge 30 feet above the water. Another girl, a wonderful swimmer I had watched enviously as she repeatedly, gracefully dived in, walked over and offered to jump with me. So she grabbed my hand, we jumped, and it turned out that was all I needed: a little bit of support from a stranger.

BELIEVING IN PEOPLE'S GOODNESS

I'm back home in London now, after I decided to take another leap and start my own business. Leaving my stable job and venturing into the unknown feels a lot like jumping into that icy rock pool: scary, exhilarating, but crucially, I now know there are people out there who want to help, who want you to succeed. All those little kindnesses from people I had never met added up, and were a big factor in my decision to go it alone. I only met those strangers for a few minutes or hours—but they changed my life.

I was very lucky to be able to travel so much last year, but I don't think opening your eyes to the potential goodness of people requires a trip to India or a vacation. It can be as simple as breaking your everyday routine, looking up and saying hello to the person who's serving your coffee in the morning instead of staring at your phone, or being brave and starting a conversation with someone new at work.

Looking back at my more cynical years earlier, I think I was scared. Opening yourself up to strangers is inherently risky; it can go wrong. It means having faith in people, which also requires trust. I'm not suggesting everyone that you meet will be a well-meaning person, that every stranger is a friend. Simply turning on the news at night or picking up a newspaper reminds me of what a harsh, hostile world we can live in. But I have learned not to be immediately on the defense when I meet someone, not to instantly shut them out. I'm more open to the possibility that they may be good, or funny, or kind—they may be those angels in disguise the Parisian bookshop hinted at. ●

TEXT **OLIVIA GAGAN** ILLUSTRATIONS **YELENA BRYKSENKOVA**

In the book 'The Unlikely Pilgrimage of Harold Fry' by Rachel Joyce, the main character, who is a very private individual, is also pleasantly surprised when he meets lots of kind strangers

HOW TO...
MAKE A PIÑATA

TEXT: CAROLINE BUIJS
ILLUSTRATION: LOUISE LOCKHART

Piñatas were originally used to chase away bad spirits. Nowadays, these brightly colored objects are a tradition at parties in many Latin American countries. The birthday boy or girl hits the piñata while blindfolded until it breaks and a flood of candy is released.

What you'll need:

wallpaper paste (from a package)   a balloon   old newspapers
scissors   craft glue   small container (for the wallpaper paste)
ribbon   crêpe paper (in different colors)   wrapped candy
other decorations (such as feathers, glitter, pompoms, etc.): optional

1. Prepare the wallpaper paste according to the instructions and place the mixture in the container. Inflate the balloon (not too full).

2. Cut or tear the old newspaper into strips and dip them in the wallpaper paste mixture.

3. Lay the strips of newspaper on the balloon but leave the knot at the top uncovered. Repeat this until there are five layers covering the balloon. Allow each layer to dry first before applying another layer on top. After you have added the last layer, let the covered balloon dry until it has hardened completely- this will take one or two days.

4 Cut the crêpe paper (while it is still rolled up) into five pieces. Make several perpendicular cuts up to the halfway mark to create fringes. Unroll the pieces of crêpe paper and glue the part without the fringes in an overlapping fashion to the piñata using the craft glue. Work from the bottom of the balloon to the top. The top of the piñata is where the knot in the balloon is. Glue other decorations to the balloon if desired.

5 Pop the balloon and remove it from the shell carefully. A hole has now been created where the knot was. Fill the piñata with candy and cover the hole with a piece of crêpe paper.

6 Poke two small holes on either side of this hole and thread the ribbon through these. Now your piñata is ready to be hung up.

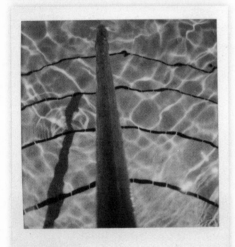

MISSING WHAT'S STILL THERE

'Anticipatory nostalgia'—that sense of sadness we feel about having to leave a beautiful place while we're still there or stop doing something wonderful before it actually ends. Hedwig Wiebes learns more about it.

There I was, at a deserted beach so vast that it seems endless, surrounded by rocky cliffs. As I descended the wooden stairs and looked around, I realized I was the only one there. Me and my two dogs, that is. Undoubtedly, this beach is jam-packed with colorful parasols and beach towels in the summer, and you'd have to squint to see the ocean through crowds of people slathered in suntan oil. But it was winter, and we had this Portuguese kingdom all to ourselves.

The dogs ran ahead in leaps and bounds as dogs do on beaches, and I looked at the happily meandering trail of paw prints that they left behind. 'I am such a lucky person,' I thought. I am currently leading a traveling life, living in a camper van, which I can combine well with my work as a writer. Thanks to this way of living, I end up in the most fabulous places at the most unexpected moments.

And then I thought: 'I have to really enjoy this a little bit more than usual as we leave tomorrow'. I'd almost forgotten about that. In fact, we were leaving this area, with its gorgeous rugged beaches, altogether. Boom, my happy feeling evaporated, and gave way to a premature sense of loss for this place that I love so much. Feeling kind of sad, I walked on—preoccupied with the imminent departure.

NOSTALGIA

Grieving for what is not there while you still have it: it feels crazy and even ungrateful. Why would you do that? And it's not very mindful either, because if you were really living 'in the moment', surely there'd be no thoughts about later or tomorrow. But the feeling can be so strong sometimes. I remember it from my childhood, too: on Saturdays I would feel free as a bird, but Sundays were filled with gloom because I was thinking about school the next day. And later I felt it again at a fantastic Florence and the Machine concert and also when I ate a most heavenly chocolate mousse with black truffles. These are all moments when I was enjoying something intensely and then suddenly stopped enjoying it, because I realized that the moment at some point would end.

However melancholy this might make one feel, it's nothing to worry about, says Tim Wildschut. He is a professor of psychology, and one of around ten people worldwide who have recently started researching this phenomenon. They call what I experienced on the beach (and so many other times) 'anticipatory nostalgia'—that is, experiencing a nostalgic feeling while the object of your nostalgia is still present. "That early sense of loss is in fact the recognition of >

Hedwig Wiebes' home is a 1985 Volkswagen camper van, in which she is currently traveling around Europe. Follow her exploits via Instagram: @hedwigwiebes, and read our interview with her in issue 19

'We like to seek out the warmth of the past when things are not going well in the present'

the fact that what you are experiencing is very special and unique," Wildschut says. "Your brain thinks ahead at such a moment and knows that this is something that you will recall with great pleasure later on. It gives you the opportunity, for example, to take a picture, or do something else that will let you capture the moment so that you can remember it better later."

MENTAL TIME TRAVEL

As the term indicates, the feeling is a specific type of nostalgia: the desire for something from the past. In the case of anticipatory nostalgia, you travel to the future in your mind and imagine the moment when you'll be thinking back to what you're experiencing right now in the present. By knowing that you will want to look back on it, your brain understands that it is worth saving this moment particularly well. This mental time travel is primarily meant to motivate yourself to, for example, create a souvenir, but at the same time it makes you already feel melancholy for the moment that will no longer be there.

The bittersweet nostalgia that you feel in these moments is not only an emotion, it also serves a practical purpose. In fact, it is a way to manage difficult moments. We like to seek out the warmth of the past when things are not going well in the present. It may seem that if you compare those two, the result might be a feeling that in the past everything was better, but what really happens is that the good things from the past give you something to hold on to, and create a feeling of trust. They show that your life is worthwhile, says American psychologist Clay Routledge in an interview in *The New York Times*. Beautiful and splendid memories give you a better feeling about the future than when you think of everyday events. It has even been proven that nostalgic feelings literally make you feel warmer.

Interestingly, nostalgia was once regarded as something negative; it was even seen as a serious neurological disease. It was Swiss doctor Johannes Hofer who first brought up the term in the 17th century. He was treating soldiers who were suffering from a mysterious disorder which disappeared like snow on a

hot summer day when he promised them that they could go home temporarily. Hofer composed the word 'nostalgia' from the ancient Greek words *nóstos* (return home) and *álgos* (which means pain), and the sensation indeed bears a great similarity to homesickness. It was only in the past decades that the difference between the two became clear when researchers found out that in the case of nostalgia we do not so much long for a place from our past, but rather for a specific moment in time—and particularly for how we felt in that moment.

No matter how well-documented these melancholy feelings may appear, very little is actually known about them. The first scientific research on anticipatory nostalgia dates back to a mere two years ago, according to Wildschut, who himself was one of the initiators of this study. "I was amazed that so little was known about this psychological state," he says, "especially as it's something that almost all of us experience every now and then. But that's the nice thing about psychology: There are still so many areas that have yet to be explored."

IN LOVE

Love is another area in which anticipatory nostalgia all too often rears its head. I was inconsolable when, as a teenager, I had to say goodbye to my long-term boyfriend because my parents got the crazy notion in their heads to emigrate to the south of France. The closer we came to saying goodbye, the more I thought about the time when we would no longer be together, even though I could still have his arms around me and I could have easily pretended the approaching future did not exist. I can also feel it sometimes for my dogs, whom I already introduced to you on the beach, when I now and then think about the fact that they will not be with me forever.

Flemish philosopher Patricia de Martelaere said, "The empty bed lies beneath every beloved". That is not only a beautiful, but also a very sad phrase. Dutch poet and philosopher Lieke Marsman elaborates on this phrase in her book *Het tegenovergestelde van een mens* >

'In the Middle Ages, melancholia was even viewed as something positive; it was seen as something profound'

(The opposite of a human being). 'It expresses how the bed in which you spend the night together simply becomes your own empty bed again when your loved one goes home, or even gets out to go to the bathroom,' she writes. 'Even finding the love of your life doesn't change that. No matter if the bed belongs to you together, and you sleep in it together in your shared bedroom, in the apartment you pay rent for together: we see the bed as the place more than any other where our symbiotic ideal of love becomes reality, but once day breaks, you both go about your own business again'.

VALUE OF LIFE
As well as the fact that the feeling of anticipatory nostalgia eventually leads to a stronger memory of the beautiful moments, experiencing the sadness of this nostalgia is not all bad. In the Middle Ages, melancholia was even viewed as something positive; it was seen as something profound, the province of writers and artists. And in Buddhism, too, this specific feeling is met with high regard. Experiencing temporality is a great thing. 'It is the impermanence of life that gives us perspective,' writes American Buddhist teacher Frank Ostaseski, an end-of-life guide and founder of a Zen hospice, in his book *The Five Invitations*. If we are not reminded of the fact that things, including life itself, will not always last, we tend to take them for granted: 'As we come in contact with life's precarious nature, we also come to appreciate its preciousness. Then we don't want to waste a minute. We want to enter our lives fully and use them in a responsible way.'

DON'T MOURN—CELEBRATE
The biggest sense of loss comes, of course, from things that will not be repeated again any time soon, maybe even ever again, like vacations and city breaks. I notice this myself, now that I have been traveling for so long and as such my life sometimes seems to be a long series of goodbyes. And although I initially thought that it wasn't good to let my thoughts fly away during a beautiful event to a moment in the future

when this lovely moment is over, I now understand its useful side. It is actually making me more mindful than ever. So let's not grieve too much over temporality, but celebrate it as the exact thing that makes life so worthwhile. ●

WANT TO READ MORE?

* 'The Five Invitations: Discovering What Death Can Teach Us About Living Fully', by Frank Ostaseski
* Visit southampton.ac.uk/nostalgia, University of Southampton's web page about the nostalgia study of Tim Wildschut et. al.
* 'The Future of Nostalgia', by Svetlana Boym

TEXT **HEDWIG WIEBES** PHOTOGRAPHY **©ALICIA BOCK/STOCKSY UNITED**

True Colors

In studying the story behind colors, journalist Caroline Buijs discovered that knowing more about color can enrich your world and encourage you to pay more attention to everything around you.

'THE PUREST AND MOST THOUGHTFUL MINDS ARE THOSE WHICH LOVE COLOR THE MOST'

John Ruskin (1819-1900), British art critic

It's strange actually, that I actually know so little about some of the things I love the most. Dahlias, for example, or ginkgos (Chinese nut trees). Danish furniture from the 1960s and jazz. But also, colors. I know that a café with a colorful décor or an elderly woman wearing a fuchsia beret (instead of the standard dull beige) can make me happy. Colorful illustrations have the same effect on me, as does a recently purchased beautiful, practical book from Japan, called *A Dictionary of Color Combinations* by artist and kimono designer, Sanzo Wada. The book consists solely of squares of color, in combinations of two, three or four hues. The colors are more muted than what I'm accustomed to, and are arranged in combinations that I wouldn't have automatically come up with myself.

My color knowledge doesn't go far beyond being able to name primary and secondary colors. What I *do* know is that blue is my favorite. I also understand that knowing more about the world around us enriches us. I had noticed this when I looked up the flowers I had seen blooming along the side of the path during my strolls through the park. It really made my walks more fun.

ITS OWN LANGUAGE

What is color, actually? Apart from being a natural phenomenon (see box below), colors are also connected to culture. You can, for example, divide color into two categories: warm and cool. We classify red and yellow as warm, and green and blue are cool. This classification hasn't even been around that long, and only dates back to the 18th century. There are actually signs that blue was viewed as being the warmest of all colors during the Middle Ages.

British design journalist Kassia St Clair wrote the book *The Secret Lives of Colour*, which is full of stories about the 75 most common shades and hues. In an email interview, she tells me about her love of colors, which started when she was young. 'My mother was a florist, so as a child I always looked at how she combined different colors in her bouquets, and she even let me try to create a few,' she writes. 'Later on, surrounded by the mahogany wainscoting in the archives of the Victoria and Albert Museum in London, UK, I did research on 18th-century English fashion and was fascinated by the colors that were all the rage back then, such as pea green.' Sometimes, St Clair says, the descriptions were accompanied by colored illustrations so that she could see what certain colors were supposed to look like, but this often wasn't the case. 'It was as if I was listening to a conversation in a language I could only half understand. I couldn't get enough of it!'

In her book, St Clair also writes about the history of colors, among other things. In the chapter entitled 'Egyptian Blue', I read how the Egyptians were 'uncommon in valuing blue: most Western cultures didn't even possess a separate word for the slice of spectrum between green and violet. For the ancient Egyptians, though, the color represented the sky, the Nile River, creation and divinity.' St Clair goes on to write, 'The color was thougt to dispel evil and bring prosperity, and was much sought after in the form of beads, which in themselves were believed to possess magical protective qualities.'

Throughout the centuries, St Clair writes, Westerners had the tendency to underestimate everything that was blue. How times have changed. Recent research conducted in ten different countries across four continents has shown that blue is by far people's favorite color; apparently, I'm not the only one. According to St Clair, in prehistoric times, shades of red, black and brown dominated; the ancient Greeks and Romans admired black, white and red, and the Romans even associated the color blue with barbarism. The tide turned in the 12th century. Aside from the fact that deep-blue,

WHAT IS COLOR?

Color is refracted light. Sunlight may be white and invisible, but this changes when it reflects off an object. What you actually see when you look at a ripe tomato or green paint for example, is light that reflects off these surfaces into your eyes. You could say that the color of an object you are looking at is the color that the object actually isn't; in other words, it is the part of the spectrum that is reflected.

Source: *The Secret Lives of Colour*, by Kassia St Clair

OFF DAY

GRANITO

WOMEN'S MARCH

FREEDOM

R IN THE MONTH

stained-glass windows could be made for a cathedral in Paris, France, for the first time, it was also around this time that the Virgin Mary was depicted increasingly frequently in a blue gown. As Mary was a particular object of reverence in the Middle Ages, the color blue also gained in popularity.

COLORFUL COMBINATIONS

In his book *Colors Demonic and Divine: Shades of Meaning in the Middle Ages and After*, Dutch author Herman Pleij observes that everything had to have a color during medieval times, more so than is now the case. Food, textiles, silk, leather, wood, illustrations in manuscripts, hair, beards and even a dog's coat: Everything was given a color. And these weren't subdued colors, but preferably bright colors in contrasting combinations. After all, during the Middle Ages colors were considered to be an important part of God's grand design: Ranks, stations and different ages were linked to specific colors. This was also very visible in clothing. On the jousting field, opponents challenged one another clad in brightly colored garments, and during church services women tried to outdo one another wearing flamboyant hues such as scarlet and crimson. Prepared from rare snails and worms, these were expensive colors.

Pleij writes that this habit of showing off with colors, however, also contributed to an unstable society 'because of the jealousy [it] provoked in the less fortunate, whose downcast state was evident from the drab, undyed clothes they wore'. The church wasn't very pleased either with all these bright colors and blamed the devil; this probably explains the rise of the colors blue and black. At the end of the Middle Ages, >

Symbolism of colors around the world

BLACK
* West: death, sorrow, luxury
* East: nobility, mystery, slyness

PURPLE
* Worldwide: mystery, spirituality
* West: fear, the unconscious, secretive, superstitious, death, dusk
* East: diabolical, sinful
* Japan: sin, fear

RED
* Worldwide: energy, strength, power, prohibition
* West: power, warmth, strength, passion, prohibition, danger
* India: creativity

YELLOW
* Worldwide: light, intellect, knowledge
* West: strength, wisdom, nervousness, tolerance
* East: authority, success, wealth

BLUE
* Worldwide: cold, calm, sadness
* West: passivity, calm, peace
* East: purity, freshness, melancholy

GREEN
* Worldwide: life, fertility, nature, energy, calm, Islam
* West: calm, fertility, fulfillment, boredom, melancholy
* China: a betrayed husband

ORANGE
* Worldwide: energy, joy
* West: sun, warmth, active, haughtiness, luxury, pride, uncertainty
* East: fashionable, pride, 'fake'

WHITE
* Worldwide: purity, peace
* West: silence, marriage, birth

Source: *The Astonishing Power of Colors*, by Jean-Gabriel Causse

GRANDMA

SPRING

JAPANESE COMBINATION

LATTE MACCHIATO

DIVE

'COLOR IS A POWER WHICH DIRECTLY INFLUENCES THE SOUL'

Wassily Kandinsky (1866-1944), Russian painter and art theorist

these colors became the colors of the court and urban aristocracies. Bright colors came to symbolize earthly delights more and more, the kinds of activities one would want to stay far away from if one believed in God. It also explains why evening wear is still primarily black.

CALM FEELING

Recently, I used my own watercolors to try out a few of the color combinations I had read about in *A Dictionary of Color Combinations*. By diluting and mixing a few of the colors in my box of paints, much to my surprise I actually came pretty close to mimicking these Japanese colors. I used the colors to paint stripes in thick brush strokes in my sketchbook, grouped according to the example set by Wada. It was all I needed for a great afternoon; this is obviously what colors can do to you. I posted the result on Instagram and, judging from the responses I received, I discovered that the book is currently popular all over the world. Illustrator Flora Waycott from Australia also has the book and due also in part to her Japanese background, was able to tell me a bit more about this. "The book focuses on color palettes from the Taishō period (1912-1926) and the start of the Shōwa period (1926-1989)," she says. "It's full of colors that are derived from the textiles (kimonos), art and literature that were part of the day-to-day life at the time. It's great to see how colors from that time seem more muted, and in spite of my Japanese background, many of the color

combinations are surprising even for me." Color combinations are very important in Japan, Waycott explains, particularly when they correspond to the seasons.

"Kimono designs and colors change with the seasons," she says. "I love the fact that so much attention has been placed on color combinations in Japan for hundreds of years. This makes these colors so refined, and the combinations are so pleasing to the eye. Mint green, light lilac and a dash of mustard yellow; this last color in particular is very Japanese. I have the feeling that colors are bolder in the West, more pronounced. Japanese colors evoke a feeling of calm."

ON POISON AND DECEIT

Returning to the popular color blue; it's the color of creativity, as French color expert Jean-Gabriel Causse writes in his book *The Astonishing Power of Colors*. According to Causse, blue represents freedom; it helps us feel fulfilled, in harmony with the world around us. He even asks us to consider the effect that a blue sky or azure ocean on the horizon has on us. Light blue, for example, makes spaces seem larger, but it is also the least edible color (remember the soup that accidentally turns blue in the movie *Bridget Jones' Diary*?). It's the only color that doesn't occur in food in nature and is subconsciously associated with poison. This is why the color blue on packaging is usually combined with a color that is reminiscent of the product inside the packaging.

And so as I ride the bus through town on a gray and cloudy day, I can't help but think about a blue ocean and a blue sky, and about the fact that the color blue symbolizes freedom; knowing this cheers me up. It's funny, but as I was reading Jane Gardam's book *Old Filth*, it suddenly struck me that the main character Betty wears a green dress when she commits adultery in Hong Kong; in China, green is the color for a husband who has been betrayed by his wife.

Learning more about color ensures that I pay more attention to the world around me. As Dutch poet and art critic K. Schippers so nicely put it, 'If you look around you, you'll notice that everything is colorful'. ●

WANT TO READ MORE?
....
* 'A Dictionary of Color
   Combinations', by Sanzo Wada
* 'The Secret Lives of Colour',
   by Kassia St Clair
* 'Colors Demonic and Divine:
   Shades of Meaning in the
   Middle Ages and After',
   by Herman Pleij
* 'The Astonishing Power of
   Colors', by Jean-Gabriel
   Causse
....

TEXT **CAROLINE BUIJS** ILLUSTRATIONS **DEBORAH VAN DER SCHAAF**

Why Accepting Help Makes Us Happier

MANY OF US FIND OFFERING HELP FAR EASIER THAN ACCEPTING IT FROM OTHERS, BUT THE LATTER CAN YIELD SO MANY BENEFITS, AS JOURNALIST CATELIJNE ELZES DISCOVERED.

When my washing machine broke, I first considered going out to find a laundromat, but decided to call my neighbor instead. This was hard for me because I don't really like asking for favors. But in this case I was in a hurry, and needed my workout clothes fast, so I decided to risk it. "Of course! You're welcome to use my machine," she said. I went to her house and we had a nice chat about where those little holes in our T-shirts come from and 90 minutes later, she was at my door with my red laundry basket, filled with clean clothes. In the course of the following week, I also did a wash at my downstairs neighbor's place. I forgot what a funny guy he is and it turns out he works at home just as often as I do—good to know. And I did the last load of laundry at my brother-in-law's who lives two blocks away from me. We drank tea while we waited for the wash to finish. We talked about his battle against the insurmountable pile of laundry he's had since he became a single father. We had a nice time.

WHAT IF THEY SAY NO?

A few days later when my machine was fixed, I felt slightly disappointed. I wondered why I don't ask for help more often, because it gave me such a good feeling. Apparently, I'm not alone in this. Research among the elderly shows that 65 percent would rather pay for help than ask family or friends. Whether this also applies to younger people hasn't been studied, but after asking friends of mine, I believe most of them don't like asking for help. According to Dutch psychologist and author Albert Sonnevelt, this is mostly because we are afraid to lose control. To start, it means handing something over to someone else, and losing our grip on it. Secondly, because asking for help requires admitting we can't do everything by ourselves. And oh how we love to be independent! Another tricky part is the feeling that you are taking on a 'debt' if you ask someone else for a favor. If they pick up your child for you from school one day, you feel like you have to return the favor some time.

There is another scary aspect to asking for help: the fear that the other person might say no. Founded by Swiss/British philosopher Alain de Botton, The School of Life has made a great animated film about this that is available on YouTube: *The Terror of a No*. In the video, a bird is walking through the forest, and would rather die than have to run into a big bad 'no'. Being told no is apparently so painful that we would rather never >

*'You aren't truly free until you can accept
that you are dependent on others'*

ask for work, money, help or even a kiss. Why? Because we have the idea that if someone says no to a request, that the no is directed at us, as a person, that we are being rejected in our entirety, even though someone is probably just saying no because it doesn't fit in with their plans.

CHANCE TO WORK TOGETHER

Managing to overcome our fear of rejection and getting over our resistance to asking for help can really do us good. This is the idea behind The School of Life's video, but also one of Sonnevelt's firm beliefs. He cites the chance to collaborate for example, which can lead to greater things. "If you want to go fast, go alone. If you want to go far, go together," he says, quoting an African proverb. "It also increases your chances of connection. Every time you ask for help or support and someone else provides this, you will become more connected to the world around you. This instills confidence. Of course we would rather do it ourselves, but this independent attitude is encouraged from the time we're young. We also really want to be part of a group, knowing that others will be there for us when we need them."

I can relate to what Sonnevelt is saying. Since that time I had to do laundry at my neighbor's, we have been in contact frequently. When her machine broke, she also knocked on my door a few times, laundry basket in hand. We now help each other make sandwiches at birthday parties. I helped her brainstorm about her

LinkedIn profile and she gave me the name of a good candidate for an interview for one of my stories. It brings people closer when you admit to needing some help and backing now and then.

American rock star Amanda Palmer, author of the book *The Art of Asking*, says very moving things about this in her TED Talk. Standing on a crate like a living statue, she talks about the time she earned her money doing that very thing. Each time someone dropped some money into her hat, she would give them a flower—'and some intense eye contact'. "I had the most profound encounters with people," she says, "especially lonely people who looked like they hadn't talked to anyone in weeks, and we would get this beautiful moment of prolonged eye contact being allowed in a city street, and we would sort of fall in love a little bit. And my eyes would say, 'Thank you. I see you'. And their eyes would say 'Nobody ever sees me. Thank you'." In this exchange, Palmer would naturally also be seen, even though she had initially asked for something, money.

This bonding experience helped Palmer master the art of asking and even raise money to record her albums through crowdfunding.

STRONG AND WISE

Asking for a favor can yield an additional benefit: making other people happy. Time after time, research has shown that doing something for someone else is one of the best things you can do if you want to be happier. By asking for

WHO HELPS WHOM?

Research has shown that our willingness to help and the type of help that we want to give is closely related to the question for whom the help is intended. We often feel this goes without saying for close family members, and for people we may not be that close to; we usually want to help the ones we like and who we know will appreciate the help. In other words, being friendly and saying thank you make a world of difference.

Source: The Netherlands Institute for Social Research (SCP)

help, you give someone else the opportunity to feel like they have a purpose, learn something new or grow. I noticed this recently when I couldn't get my car (which doesn't have power steering) out of a tight parking space and I asked a charming young man for help. Seemingly effortlessly, he extricated my car from the space and I watched him cycle off with a smile on his face. We were two happy people.

According to Sonnevelt, we can also grow as a result of asking for help, particularly if it's something we find daunting. "When you look for support, you are essentially taking control," Sonnevelt says. "You don't just resign yourself passively to your fate, for example if you can't do something or are exhausted from always trying to do everything yourself. You are showing that you are aware of what you can and can't do. This is being strong and wise." But can't we also grow by *not* asking for help? "Yes, but this comes at a price," Sonnevelt says. "I often see people in my practice who don't want help from others out of some kind of stubbornness or pride, and get burned out. I see it a lot with parents and independent contractors. Let others help you. It can really cut down on the mountain of stress and everything you have on your plate. It may seem like the ultimate form of freedom, not needing anyone, but I believe you aren't truly free until you can accept that you are dependent on others."

I have found there's another benefit to accepting help; I believe it makes me a nicer person. Acknowledging that I   >

'Don't forget, if your request does get rejected, your heart will continue to beat. It won't kill you'

am vulnerable in some ways and can really use some help means that I am more open to the rest of the world. It can't be a coincidence that people ask me for help more often now and I also offer it more frequently. We're in this together!

PAT ON THE BACK

All these benefits are great, but what if you're still afraid to ask for help? In her book *Help Is Not a Four-letter Word*, American author Peggy Collins recommends using the ACT formula, which consists of three parts:
1. Ask yourself each time what you're afraid of (Afraid). This makes you more aware of what's stopping you from asking for help.

2. Abandon the idea that you should be able to manage everything (Control) and that asking for something means that you have immediately lost all control.
3. Learn to have faith in the situation and take the risk that you can also trust the other person (Trust).

   "Whether it's about asking for help or delegating tasks in your work, what it boils down to is that you have to let something go: your conviction about how something should be done, your sense of responsibility or your supposed independence," Sonnevelt says. "Letting go hurts and can be scary. You can't move forward until you acknowledge this fear or are able to view it with compassion. Once you've done this, you can start practicing. Start by asking for something small for which you know the chance of getting a yes is fairly high. Make it a sort of routine; come up with one small thing every day you could ask for help with, such as 'Can you read this text for me?' or 'Can you give me advice on the best way to respond to this email?' Reward yourself when you succeed, give yourself a pat on the back. This helps your brain produce substances that give you a good feeling and your victory will stay fresh in your mind longer. And don't forget, if your request does get rejected, your heart will continue to beat. It won't kill you. The more often you experience this, the better you'll be at it." ●

THIS CAN HELP

Belgian psychologist Nathalie Cardinaels offers the following 'helping thoughts' to enable us to ask for or accept help:

* Even the strongest person in the group, the most stable rock, needs help now and then. This has nothing to do with weakness but with being human.
* You might be afraid to ask for help because you don't want to be a burden to others. However, the other person really will say so if it's not convenient for them (at that time).
* The other person might actually see it as a compliment that you're asking them for help. This means that you see and value their insight and capabilities.
* If someone offers to help, you just say yes even if you're thinking 'I can do it myself'. Why not just wait and see what the benefits are?

TEXT **CATELIJNE ELZES** PHOTOGRAPHY **MARGRIET HOEKSTRA** STYLING **ANNEMIEKE PAARLBERG** MAKE-UP **CARMEN ZOMERS@YVESROCHER** HAND-LETTERING **VALESCA VAN WAVEREN**

FLOW DIARY 2019

Weekly Notebook 2019

flow

With bookmark ribbon and elastic band

Artwork by Dinara Mirtalipova

EXTRAS: stickers, postcards, paper clips

August

Week-to-view

Opening a brand new diary is always a magical moment: a new year ahead of you, with lots of empty pages that remind you that everything is still possible. Soon, those blank pages will no doubt be full of appointments, lists, fun things to do, surprises, chores and vacations. But wouldn't it be great if some of those pages stay empty? It might not always be possible—daily life tends to catch up with you—but how about trying to resist the urge to fill in every hour of every day? Because, if you keep running all the time, you may miss all the beautiful yet unplanned things along the way. We hope your diary will be full of lots of exciting plans—as well as the occasional empty page, of course. Good luck!

The Flow Diary 2019 is illustrated by US-based Dinara Mirtalipova, a self-taught artist originally from Uzbekistan.

THE FLOW DIARY 2019 (15 X 20 CM / 5.9 X 7.9 INCH) COSTS €16.95 AND IS AVAILABLE FROM THE FLOW WEB SHOP. GO TO FLOWMAGAZINE.COM/DIARY2019 TO ORDER YOUR COPY.

Drawing Plants

THERE ARE SO MANY THINGS TO NOTICE WHEN YOU ARE DRAWING

PLANTS—NOT ONLY THE COLORS AND THE SHAPES, BUT ALSO THE

TEXTURES, THE POT HOLDING THE PLANT AND SO ON. WE

ASKED NINE ILLUSTRATORS TO DRAW THEIR FAVORITE PLANT

AND GIVE ONE TIP ON HOW TO BEST DRAW YOUR OWN.

RUBY TAYLOR: APHELANDRA SQUARROSA

"Look at the negative space between the leaves—that will help to get the shape of the leaves right. Also be bold with color."

➠ **Instagram:** @rubyst
➠ Ruby-taylor.co.uk

JENNIFER ORKIN LEWIS: FICUS LYRATA

"Look carefully at the shape of the leaves and the way they overlap."

➠ **Instagram:** @augustwren
➠ Augustwren.com

LOTTE DIRKS: MARANTA

"Use various layers on top of each other, preferably mixing materials. This gives your drawing some life. You could first use ink to apply an even layer of color, for example, and then add details in paint using a thin-tipped paintbrush later."

➠ **Instagram:** @lottedirks ➠ Greenhouseprints.com

DINARA MIRTALIPOVA: DIEFFENBACHIA

"First start with drawing the stems, then add wide leaves here and there. The beautiful pattern on the leaves can be painted using darker and lighter shades of green. And don't forget the pot, which you can decorate how you want."

●◇ **Instagram:** @mirdinara ●◇ Mirdinara.com

SARA ROCHA: ANTHURIUM

"Study the whole plant in detail first. Next, draw it out very lightly in pencil. Choose your color palette and then paint the plant in a layer-based technique, adding the shades and highlights at the end."

●◇ **Instagram:**
@sararrochaillustration
●◇ Sararrocha.etsy.com

KATE PUGSLEY: FICUS ELASTICA

"I like to paint plants without any planning beforehand. Painting several quick watercolor or gouache sketches on a page usually results in at least one or two that look fresh, interesting and spontaneous."

●◇ **Instagram:** @katepugsley ●◇ Katepugsley.com

BRIE HARRISON: CHLOROPHYTUM COMOSUM

"Think of drawing a plant as being similar to a portrait. I don't think it's necessarily about capturing the preciseness of the leaf and stem, but about giving the plant a personality."

●◆ **Instagram:** @brieharrison ●◆ Brieharrison.com

ELIZABETH BARNETT: MONSTERA

"Drawing from life helps you get different angles and perspective on the plant you are illustrating. Include the veins and roots to give it depth."

●◆ **Instagram:** @elizabethbarnett
●◆ Elizabethbarnett.com

ANNE BENTLEY: YUCCA

"I pay special attention to the negative space when drawing plants, and sometimes exaggerate it to make the composition more interesting."

●◆ **Instagram:** @annembentley
●◆ Annembentley.com

HAVE A GO
DIY

INSPIRED BY OUR
ILLUSTRATORS' TIPS?

DRAW YOUR OWN
PLANT HERE

flow

Allie slow

bad
hand

good hand

Zoey
Zoey

good

hand

I

I ♥ Zoey
Zoey

bad hand

Allie

bad
hand